Edited by Alan Durband

PLAYBILL ONE

Hutchinson Educational

HUTCHINSON EDUCATIONAL LTD
178–202 Great Portland Street, London W1

London Melbourne Sydney
Auckland Johannesburg Cape Town
and agencies throughout the world

First published 1969
Second impression 1970

Printed in Great Britain by litho on smooth wove paper
by Anchor Press, and bound by Wm. Brendon,
both of Tiptree, Essex

ISBN 0 09 105400 1 (c)
0 09 105401 x (p)

Playbill One

The *Playbill* series brings together new, specially commissioned or adapted plays for use in schools. The emphasis is on contemporary developments in the theatre and allied media. The volumes are graded in difficulty.

Books by Alan Durband

ENGLISH WORKSHOP 1–3

CONTEMPORARY ENGLISH 1–2

SHORTER CONTEMPORARY ENGLISH

NEW ENGLISH 1–4

Edited by Alan Durband

NEW DIRECTIONS

Five one-act plays in the modern idiom

PLAYBILL TWO

PLAYBILL THREE

Contents

Introduction

Playbill One contains plays by Alan Ayckbourn, David Campton, David Cregan, Beverley Cross and Donald Howarth.

1 *The Plays*

Alan Ayckbourn's *Ernie's Incredible Illucinations* is a bright comedy based on the extraordinary powers of Ernie Fraser, a day-dreamer with a difference. Like all schoolboys Ernie has a vivid imagination, but Ernie's thoughts have a disturbing habit of turning into reality. After a number of embarrassing episodes, Ernie's parents decide to consult a doctor, who is sceptical. Several of Ernie's adventures are acted out for us in flashback, but when Ernie fails to produce a Brass Band on demand, the doctor diagnoses group hallucination and recommends a visit to a specialist. However, 'Ernie's incredible illucinations' aren't to be dismissed quite so lightly, as you will see. . . .

'You have to be hard to get to the right place.' Adam, in David Campton's play *The Right Place,* is ruthlessly hard. He knows what he wants and intends to get it. Adam's pilgrimage is one of discomfort and hardship, yet he struggles on in spite of the temptations that befall him. He sacrifices everything for his goal—not even the bonds of friendship or compassion will deflect him from his purpose. Eventually he reaches the Right Place, only to find that those who journeyed with him have reached there first and found happiness before him. The moral? With the help of Hughie you should be able to work this out.

Arthur, by David Cregan, is the saga of Arthur Parsons, who fights for his independence at the advanced age of twenty-one by smashing crockery and setting fire to his aunt's home. Naturally, this involves him in a clash with the authorities—the Fire Brigade, the Police, and the local Mayor—and to make matters more complicated it also involves him in Trying to Go Out with Girls. Arthur grows in heroic stature as the play proceeds. He overthrows the fascist Mayor, wins a worthy bride, and emerges as a new, noble Arthur Parsons, with a glorious past and a promising political future.

The politics of Beverley Cross's *The Crickets Sing* belong to the seventeenth century, when England was in the throes of a civil war. The hero of the play is Orlando Nokes, a Dramatic Author, who has been out of touch with national politics for three years. Unfortunately, he returns to London with his masterpiece at a time when drama of any kind is against the law. To avoid having his ears nailed to a pillory—the usual punishment for writing plays—he agrees to take part in a Roundhead plot, but when this turns out to be something much more villainous than an attack on the Royal Mint, Nokes makes use of his skill as an actor to save the life of King Charles I.

Donald Howarth's *School Play* also has moments of menace, as when the ciphers gang up against the individualist, Six. This is a scripted play with opportunities for improvisation. There are so many parts that every member of the class, including your teacher, will be involved and must keep alert: you will probably need plenty of rehearsal before you can run through smoothly from beginning to end. In tackling this experimental play and bringing it to life you will be experiencing some of the problems of actors and producers in the modern theatre.

2 *The Playwrights*

Alan Ayckbourn was born in Hampstead, London, in 1939. Since leaving school he has worked as stage-manager, actor, writer and director. He first began to write plays whilst working with the late Stephen Joseph's Theatre-in-the-Round at Scarborough and Stoke-on-Trent; *Relatively Speaking,* his first play to be produced in London, opened at the Duke of York's Theatre in March 1967 and had a long and successful run both there and in the provinces. Alan Ayckbourn is at present working with the BBC as a radio drama producer, encouraging new writing talent. He is married to a former actress and has two children.

David Campton is another product of the Theatre-in-the-Round company. He was born over a barber's shop in Leicester, where he still lives, in 1924. For eight years he was a clerk with the local education authority. For another seven he worked for the East Midlands Gas Board. During this period he 'learned how to write', and in 1956 became a professional playwright, working as actor and dramatist for Stephen Joseph. His many TV and stage plays (one of which, *Out of the Flying Pan,* is published in the Hutchinson collection *New Directions*) have been widely performed in Europe and the USA. Some of his radio work is regularly used in language-teaching programmes as far afield as Russia and the Middle East.

David Cregan was born in 1931, the fourth of four sons of a Manchester shirt manufacturer. After National Service as a corporal in the RAF he took a degree at Clare College, Cambridge. He taught for two years in Palm Beach, Florida, and on returning to England was 'an unhappy teacher in Manchester', a salesman for mouse poison, a clerk at the AA, and finally a very happy teacher in Hertfordshire. His first novel appeared in 1959, his first play, *Miniatures,* i1n965 . In 1966 he won the

C. H. Foyle Award for the best play of the year with *The Dancers* and *Transcending*. On the strength of an Arts Council grant he became a full-time writer in 1967. He is married with one son.

Beverley Cross, born in 1931, was educated at the Nautical College, Pangbourne, and Balliol College, Oxford. After service in the British Army and the Norwegian Merchant Service he joined the Stratford Memorial Theatre company as an actor, staying for two seasons. His first play, *One More River*, was produced in Liverpool and London in 1958; two children's plays followed—*The Singing Dolphin* and *The Three Cavaliers*—and in 1960 he was awarded an Arts Council bursary. In 1961 his adaptation and translation of *Boeing-Boeing* (the longest-running comedy on the London stage) opened at the Apollo Theatre. Since then Beverley Cross has written several screen plays, television plays, and libretti—plus the books of two successful musicals, *Half a Sixpence* and *Jorrocks*. Beverley Cross lives in Hertfordshire.

Donald Howarth was born in 1931, the son of a professional soldier. After an apprenticeship to a signwriter he turned to the theatre, spending five years in repertory as actor and stage-manager. Then he left the theatre and took a variety of jobs—as a clerk in a sausage factory, a barman, a chip cook, a counter hand in a coffee-bar, a bric-à-brac stallholder, and a laundry-man on a Dutch liner. He began to write when at sea, for something to do. His first play *Sugar in the Morning,* written in under three weeks, was produced at the Royal Court Theatre, Sloane Square, in 1958. It won a prize in the Encyclopaedia Britannica competition and was televised. Subsequently, encouraged by Cecil Clarke of Globe Productions, he wrote *A Lily in Little India*, *Ogodiveleftthegason*, and an adaptation of L. P. Hartley's *The Go-Between*. He now directs plays as a holiday from writing them, and writes film scripts. *School Play* is his tenth play.

Acknowledgements

For permission to reprint the plays in this volume the editor is grateful to the following authors and their agents:
Alan Ayckbourn and Margaret Ramsey Ltd for *Ernie's Incredible Illucinations*; David Campton and ACTAC (Theatrical and Cinematic) Ltd for *The Right Place*; David Cregan and Margaret Ramsey Ltd for *Arthur*; Beverley Cross and Curtis Brown Ltd for *The Crickets Sing*; Donald Howarth and Margaret Ramsay Ltd for *School Play*.

Ernie's Incredible Illucinations

ALAN AYCKBOURN

CAST

ERNIE
MUM
DAD
RECEPTIONIST
DOCTOR
OFFICER
AUNTIE MAY
1ST BARKER
2ND BARKER
3RD BARKER
4TH BARKER
REFEREE
TIMEKEEPER
MAN
WOMAN
KID SARACEN
2ND MAN
LADY
ATTENDANT
TRAMP
GIRL LIBRARIAN
LADY LIBRARIAN
PATIENTS, SOLDIERS, CROWDS, BOXERS, etc.

Ernie's Incredible Illucinations

SCENE: *At one side of the stage—a doctor's waiting room. It is filled with an assortment of miserable-looking patients, coughing, wheezing, sneezing and moaning. Amongst them sit* MR *and* MRS FRASER *and their son* ERNIE.

ERNIE [*to audience, after a second*]: If you ever want to feel ill—just go and spend a happy half-hour in a doctor's waiting room. If you're not ill when you get there, you will be when you leave.

[*A man enters, having seen the doctor. He is moaning. He crosses the waiting room and goes out. The other patients look at him and sorrowfully shake their heads.*
The RECEPTIONIST *enters*]

RECEPTIONIST: Mr and Mrs Fraser . . . [MUM *and* DAD *rise*] Doctor will see you now.

MUM: Thank you. Come on, Ernie.

[MUM *and* DAD *and* ERNIE *follow the* RECEPTIONIST *across the stage to the* DOCTOR *who sits behind a table*]

MUM: 'Morning, Doctor.

[RECEPTIONIST *leaves*]

DOCTOR: Ah. Ah. Mr and Mrs Fraser. Is that it?

MUM: That's right. I'm Mrs Fraser . . . and this is my husband, Mr Fraser . . . and this is our son . . . Ernie.

DOCTOR: Ah yes. Ernie. I've been hearing all sorts of things about you, young Ernie. Now, what have you been up to, eh?

DAD: Illucinations.

DOCTOR: I beg your pardon?

DAD: Illucinations.

DOCTOR: Oh, yes illuci—quite, yes.

MUM: What my husband means doctor is that Ernie has been creating these illusions.

DOCTOR: Ah.

MUM: Well, they're more than illusions, really.

DAD: I'll say.

DOCTOR: Beg pardon?

DAD: I'll say.

MUM: He's been causing that much trouble. At school, at home, everywhere he goes. I mean we can't go on like this. His Dad's not as strong as he was, are you, Albert?

DAD: No.

DOCTOR: What?

DAD: No.

DOCTOR: Perhaps it would be better if you told me a little more about it. When did you first notice this . . . ?

MUM: Ah well . . .

DAD: Ah.

MUM: Now then . . .

DAD: Now . . .

MUM: He'd have been . . . well, it'd have been about . . . near enough . . . er . . .

DOCTOR: Go on.

[ERNIE *steps forward. During his speech* MUM *and* DAD *remain seated. The* DOCTOR *moves to the side of the stage, produces a notebook and makes notes on what follows*]

ERNIE: It started with these daydreams. You know, the sort everybody gets. Where you suddenly score a hat trick in the last five minutes of the Cup Final or you bowl out the West Indies for ten runs . . . or saving your granny from a blazing helicopter, all that sort of rubbish.

It was one wet Saturday afternoon and me and my Mum and my Dad were all sitting about in the happy home having one of those exciting afternoon rave-ups we usually have in our house.

[ERNIE *sits at the table in the* DOCTOR'S *chair and starts to read a book.* MUM *has started knitting and* DAD *just sits, gazing ahead of him. A long silence*]

ERNIE: It was all go in our house.

[*Pause*]

MUM: I thought you'd be at the match today, Albert.

DAD: Not today.

MUM: Not often you miss a game.

DAD: They're playing away.

MUM: Oh.

DAD: In Birmingham. I'm damned if I'm going to Birmingham. Even for United.

ERNIE: Meanwhile . . . while this exciting discussion was in progress, I was reading this book about the French wartime resistance workers and of the dangers they faced . . . often arrested in their homes. I started wondering what would happen if a squad of soldiers turned up at our front door, having been tipped off about the secret radio transmitter hidden in our cistern . . . when suddenly . . .

[*The tramp of feet, and a squad of soldiers comes marching on and up to their front door*]

OFFICER: 'Halte!' [*He bangs on the door*]

[*Pause*]

DAD: That the door?

MUM: What?

DAD: The door.

MUM: Was it?

OFFICER: Open zis door. Open the door! [*He knocks again*]

MUM: Oh, that'll be the milkman wanting his money. He always comes round about now. Albert, have you got ten bob . . . ?

DAD [*fumbling in his pockets*]: Ah . . .

OFFICER [*shouting*]: Open zis door immediately. Or I shall order my men to break it down. [*He bangs on the door again*]

MUM: Just a minute. Coming.

DAD: Should have one somewhere . . .

OFFICER: We know you're in there, English spy! Come out with your hands up . . .

MUM: What's he shouting about? Oh, I'd better ask him for three pints next week, if Auntie May's coming . . .

OFFICER: Zis is your last chance . . . [*He knocks again*]

MUM: Oh shut up . . .

[*The* OFFICER *signals his men. Two of them step back, brace their shoulders and prepare to charge the door*]

MUM: I'm coming . . . I'm coming.

ERNIE: I shouldn't go out there, Mum . . .

MUM: What?

ERNIE: I said don't go out there . . .

MUM: What—

ERNIE: It's not the milkman. It's a squad of enemy soldiers . . .

MUM: Who?

ERNIE: They've come for me . . .

MUM: Who has?

ERNIE: The soldiers. They've found out about the radio transmitter . . .

MUM: What radio?

DAD: Hey, here, that's a point. Have you paid our telly licence yet, Ethel? It might be the detector van.

MUM: Oh, sit down, Albert. Stop worrying. It's just Ernie. Shut up, Ernie.

ERNIE: But Mum . . .

DAD: I think I'll take the telly upstairs. Just in case . . .

[*The soldiers charge at the door. A loud crash*]

ERNIE: Don't go out, Mum.

MUM: Shut up.

DAD [*struggling with the set*]: Just take it upstairs.

ERNIE: Don't go.

MUM: I can't leave him out there. The way he's going he'll have the door off its hinges in a minute . . . [*She moves to the door*]

DAD: Mind your backs. Out of my way . . .

ERNIE: Mum . . .

[MUM *opens the door just as the two soldiers are charging for the second time. They shoot past her, straight into the hall, collide with* DAD *and land in a heap with him.* DAD *manages to hold the TV set above his head and save it from breaking*]

MUM: Hey . . .

DAD: Oy!

[*The* OFFICER *and the other soldiers enter.* ERNIE *crouches behind the table*]

OFFICER: Ah-ha! The house is surrounded.

MUM: Who are you?

OFFICER: Put up your hands. My men will search the house.

DAD [*feebly*]: Hey . . .

OFFICER [*shouting up the stairs*]: We know you're hiding in here, you can't get away . . .

DAD: Hey . . . *hey* . . . HEY!

OFFICER: Ah-ha. What have we here?

DAD: Oh. It's the telly. The neighbour's telly. Not mine.

OFFICER: Ah-ha.

DAD: Just fixing it for him, you see . . .

OFFICER: Outside.

DAD: Eh?

OFFICER: You will come with me.

DAD: What, in this? I'm not going out in this rain.

OFFICER: Outside or I shoot.

DAD: Here . . .

MUM: Albert . . .

ERNIE: Hold it. Drop those guns.

OFFICER: Ah, so . . . [*he raises his gun*]

ERNIE: Da-da-da-da-da-da-da-da-da-da-da.

[*The soldiers collapse and are strewn all over the hall.* MUM *screams. Then a silence*]

MUM: Oh, Ernie. What have you done?

ERNIE: Sorry, Mum.

DAD: Oh, lad . . .

MUM: Are they—dead?

DAD: Yes.

[MUM *screams again*]

DAD: Steady, steady. This needs thinking about.

MUM: What about the neighbours?

DAD: Could create a bit of gossip, this could.

MUM: What about the carpet? Look at it.

DAD: Hasn't done that much good.

MUM: What'll we do with them?

DAD: Needs a bit of thinking about.

[ERNIE *steps forward. As he speaks and during the next section,* DAD *and* MUM *carry off the bodies*]

ERNIE: Well, Mum and Dad decided that the best thing to do was to pretend it hadn't happened. That was usually the way they coped with all emergencies . . .

[DOCTOR *steps forward*]

MUM [*struggling with a body*]: We waited till it got dark, you see . . .

DOCTOR: Yes? And then . . . ?

DAD: We dumped 'em.

DOCTOR: I beg your pardon?

DAD: We dumped 'em. Took 'em out and dumped 'em.

DOCTOR: Dumped them? Where, for heaven's sake?

DAD: Oh . . . bus shelters . . . park benches . . .

MUM: Corporation car park.

DAD: Left one in the all-night cafeteria.

MUM: And one in the Garden of Rest.

DAD: Caused a bit of a rumpus.

DOCTOR: I'm not surprised.

MUM: We had the police round our way for days—trying to sort it out . . .

DAD: They never did get to the bottom of it, though.

DOCTOR: Extraordinary. And then?

ERNIE [*stepping forward*]: And then—Auntie May arrived to stay. I liked my Auntie May.

[AUNTIE MAY *enters.* DOCTOR *steps back again*]

AUNTIE: 'Ullo, Ernie lad. Have a sweetie.

ERNIE: Ta, Auntie. And Auntie May took me to the fair.

[*The stage is filled with jostling people, barkers and fairground music*]

1ST BARKER: Yes, indeed, the world's tallest man! He's so tall, madam, his breakfast is still sliding down him at tea time. Come along now, sir. Come inside now . . .

2ND BARKER [*simultaneously*]: Ladies and Gentlemen. I am prepared to guarantee that you will never again, during your lifetimes, see anything as unbelievably amazing as the Incredible Porcupine Woman. See her quills and get your thrills. Direct from the unexplored South American Jungle . . .

3RD BARKER: Try your luck . . . come along, Madam . . . leave your husband there, dear, he'll still be there when you come back . . . tell you what—if he isn't I can sell you a replacement . . . five shots for sixpence . . . knock 'em all down and pick up what you like . . .

ERNIE: Can I have a go on that, Auntie?

AUNTIE: Not now, Ernie.

ERNIE: Oh go on, Auntie May.

AUNTIE: I want a cup of tea.

ERNIE: Have an ice cream.

AUNTIE: I've had three. I can't have any more. It'll bring on my condition . . .

ERNIE: What condition, Auntie?

AUNTIE: Never you mind what. But I should never have had that candy floss as well. I'll suffer for it.

4TH BARKER: Just about to start, Ladies and Gentlemen. A heavyweight boxing bout, featuring the one and only unofficial challenger for the heavyweight championship of the world—Kid Saracen. The Kid will be fighting this afternoon, for the very first time, a demonstration contest against the new sensation from Tyneside, Eddie 'Grinder' Edwards. In addition, Ladies and Gentlemen, the Kid is offering fifty pounds—yes, fifty pounds—to any challenger who manages to last three three-minute rounds . . .

ERNIE: Oh, come on Auntie. Let's go in and watch.

AUNTIE: What is it?

ERNIE: Boxing.

AUNTIE: Boxing? I'm not watching any boxing. I don't mind wrestling but I'm not watching boxing. It's bloodthirsty.

ERNIE: Auntie . . .

AUNTIE: Nasty stuff, boxing . . .

4TH BARKER: Come along, lady. Bring in the young gentleman. Let him see the action . . .

AUNTIE: Oh no . . .

4TH BARKER: Come along . Two is it?

ERNIE: Yes please. Two.

4TH BARKER: Thank you, son.

AUNTIE: Eh?

ERNIE: This way, Auntie.

[*Before* AUNTIE MAY *can protest, she and* ERNIE *are inside the boxing booth. The crowd have formed a square around the ring in which stand* KID SARACEN, EDDIE EDWARDS *and the* REFEREE]

REF: Ladies and Gentlemen, introducing on my right, the ex-unofficial challenger for the World Heavyweight Championship—KID SARACEN . . .

[*Boos from the crowd*]

And on my left the challenger from Newcastle upon Tyne . . . EDDIE EDWARDS . . .

[*Crowd cheers*]

[*To boxers*] Right, I want a good clean fight, lads. No low blows and when I say break stop boxing right away. Good luck.

TIMEKEEPER: Seconds out—

[The bell rings. The crowd cheers as the boxers size each other up. They mostly cheer on EDWARDS*—'Come on, Eddie' 'Murder him, Eddie', etc. Boxers swap a few punches]*

AUNTIE: Oooh. I can't look.

[The man next to her starts cheering]

MAN: Flatten him, Eddie.

*[*AUNTIE *peers out from behind her hands in time to see the* KID *clout* EDDIE *fairly hard]*

AUNTIE: Hey, you stop that.

MAN: Get at him, Eddie . . .

AUNTIE: Yes, that's right, get at him.

MAN: Hit him.

AUNTIE: Knock him down.

MAN: Smash him.

AUNTIE: Batter him. *[She starts to wave her arms about in support of* EDDIE, *throwing punches at the air]*

MAN: That's it, missis. You show 'em.

AUNTIE: I would, I would.

MAN: Give 'em a run for their money, would you?

AUNTIE: I'm not that old . . .

MAN: Eddie!

AUNTIE: Come on, Eddie!

ERNIE: Eddie!

[*In the ring* KID *throws a terrific blow which brings* EDDIE *to his knees*]

REF: One . . . two . . . three . . .

MAN: Get up, Eddie . . .

AUNTIE: Get up . . . get up . . .

REF:. . . four . . .

[EDDIE *rises and blunders round the ring. The* KID *knocks him clean out.*

The REFEREE *counts him out. Crowd boos wildly. The* KID *walks smugly round the ring, his hands raised above his head in triumph*]

AUNTIE: You brute.

MAN: Boo. Dirty fight . . .

AUNTIE: Bully . . .

REF [*quietening the crowd*]: And now—Ladies and Gentlemen, the Kid wishes to issue a challenge to any person here who would like to try his skill at lasting three rounds . . . any person here. Come along now . . . anybody care to try . . .

[*Muttering from the crowd*]

AUNTIE [*to the* MAN]: Go on then.

MAN: Who, me?

AUNTIE: What are you frightened of, then?

MAN: I'm frightened of him . . .

REF: Come along now. We're not asking you to do it for nothing. We're offering fifty pounds . . . fifty pounds, gentlemen . . .

AUNTIE: Go on. Fifty quid.

MAN: I'd need that to pay the hospital bill . . .

AUNTIE: Go on . . .

MAN: It's all right for you, lady . . . just standing there telling other people to go and get their noses broken.

AUNTIE: All right, then. I'll go in myself. Excuse me . . . [*She starts to push through the crowd towards the ring*]

MAN: Hey . . .

ERNIE: Auntie, where are you going?

AUNTIE: Out of my way . . .

MAN: Hey, stop her . . . she's off her nut . . .

ERNIE: Auntie!

AUNTIE [*hailing the referee*]: Hey, you . . .

REF: Hallo, lady, what can we do for you? Come to challenge him, have you?

[*Laughter from the crowd*]

AUNTIE: That's right. Help me in.

REF: Just a minute, lady, you've come the wrong way for the jumble sale, this is a boxing ring . . .

AUNTIE: I know what it is. Wipe that silly smile off your face. Come on then, rings out of your seconds . . .

[*Crowd cheers*]

REF: Just a minute. Just a minute. What do you think you're playing at . . . ?

AUNTIE: You said anyone could have a go, didn't you?

WOMAN: That's right. Give her a go, then.

REF [*getting worried*]: Now, listen . . .

KID SARACEN: Go home. There's a nice old lady . . .

[*Crowd boos*]

AUNTIE: You cheeky ha'porth.

2ND MAN: Hit him, Grandma.

[*Crowd shouts agreement*]

REF: Tell you what, folks. Let's give the old lady ten shillings for being a good sport . . .

AUNTIE: I don't want your ten bob . . . Come on.

WOMAN: Get the gloves on, Granny.

AUNTIE: I don't need gloves. My hands have seen hard work. I was scrubbing floors before he was thought of . . .

WOMAN: That's right, love.

ERNIE [*stepping forward*]: And then suddenly I got this idea. Maybe Auntie May could be the new heavyweight champion of the world . . .

[*The bell rings.* AUNTIE MAY *comes bouncing out of her corner flinging punches at* THE KID *who looks startled. Crowd cheers*]

AUNTIE: Let's have you.

KID SARACEN: Hey, come off it!

[REF *tries vainly to pull* AUNTIE *back but she dances out of reach*]

KID SARACEN: Somebody chuck her out.

[KID *turns to appeal to the crowd.* AUNTIE *punches him in the back*]

AUNTIE: Gotcher.

KID SARACEN: Ow!

[AUNTIE *bombards the* KID *with punches*]

ERNIE [*commentator style*]: And Auntie May moves in again and catches the Kid with a left and a right to the body and there's a right cross to the head—and that really hurt him—and it looks from here as if the champ is in real trouble . . . as this amazing sixty-eight-year-old challenger follows up with a series of sharp left jabs . . . one, two, three, four jabs . . .

[*The* KID *is reeling back*]

And then, bang, a right hook and he's down . . .

[KID *goes down on his knees. Crowd cheers*]

AUNTIE [*to* REF]: Go on. Start counting.

CROWD: One—two—three—four—five—six . . .

[*The* KID *gets up again*]

ERNIE: And the Kid's on his feet but he's no idea where he is . . . and there's that tremendous right uppercut . . . and he's down again . . .

[CROWD *counts him out.* AUNTIE *dances round the ring with glee. The crowd bursts into the ring and* AUNTIE *is lifted on to their shoulders. They go out singing 'For she's a jolly good fellow'.* REFEREE *and* THE KID *are left*]

REF: Come on. Get up—Champ.

KID SARACEN: Ooooh. [*He staggers to his feet*]

[KID *goes out supported by the* REFEREE. ERNIE, DAD, MUM *and the* DOCTOR *are left*]

DOCTOR [*still writing, excitedly*]: Absolutely incredible!

MUM: Terrible it was. It took it out of her, you know. She was laid up all Sunday.

DAD: And we had all those fellows round from the Amateur Boxing Association trying to sign her up to fight for the Combined Services.

MUM: So I told his Dad on the Monday, seeing as it was half term, 'Take him somewhere where he won't get into trouble,' I said. 'Take him somewhere quiet.'

DAD: So I took him down to the library.

[DOCTOR *retires to the side of the stage again.* DAD, MUM *and* ERNIE *exit.*

The scene becomes the Public Library. It is very quiet. Various people tip-toe about. At one end sits an intellectual-looking lady with glasses, reading; at the other, an old tramp eating his sandwiches from a piece of newspaper. One or two others. A uniformed attendant walks up and down importantly.

The LADY WITH GLASSES *looks up at the lights. She frowns*]

LADY: Excuse me . . .

ATTENDANT: Sssshhh!

LADY: Sorry. [*Mouthing silently*] The light's gone.

ATTENDANT [*mouthing*]: What?

LADY [*whispering*]: I said the light's gone over here.

ATTENDANT [*whispering*]: What?

LADY: New bulb.

ATTENDANT [*shakes his head not understanding*]

LADY [*loudly*]: UP THERE! YOU NEED A NEW BULB—IT'S GONE. I CAN'T SEE.

PEOPLE: Sssshhhh!

ATTENDANT [*whispering*]: Right.

LADY [*whispering*]: Thank you.

[ATTENDANT *tip-toes out as* DAD *and* ERNIE *tip-toe in*]

DAD [*to* ERNIE]: Sssshhhh!

[ERNIE *nods. They tip-toe and sit*]

ERNIE [*to audience*]: I didn't really think much of this idea of my Mum's . . .

PEOPLE: Ssssshhhh!

ERNIE [*whispering*]: I didn't really think much of this idea of my Mum's. It was a bit like sitting in a graveyard only not as exciting. The trouble is, in library reading rooms some bloke's pinched all the best magazines already and you're left with dynamic things like *The Pig Breeder's Monthly Gazette* and suchlike. I'd got stuck with *The Bell Ringer's Quarterly*. Which wasn't one of my hobbies. Nobody else seemed to be enjoying themselves either. Except the bloke eating his sandwiches in the corner. I reckoned he wasn't a tramp at all, but a secret agent heavily disguised, waiting to pass on some secret documents to his contact who he was to meet in the library and who was at this very moment lying dead in the Reference Section, a knife in his ribs. Realising this, the tramp decides to pick on the most trustworthy-looking party in the room . . . My Dad!

[*The* TRAMP *gets up stealthily and moves over to* DAD. *As he passes him he knocks his magazine out of his hand*]

DAD: Hey!

TRAMP: Beg pardon mister. [*He bends to pick up the magazine and hands it back to* DAD. *As he does so he thrusts his newspaper parcel into* DAD*'s hands*]

TRAMP: Sssshhhh. Take this. Quickly. They're watching me. Guard it with your life.

DAD: Eh?

[TRAMP *hurries away. A sinister man in a mackintosh gets up and follows him out*]

DAD: Who the heck was that?

ERNIE: Dunno, Dad.

DAD [*examining the parcel*]: What's all this, then?

ERNIE: Dunno.

DAD: I don't want his sandwiches. Spoil my dinner. [*As he unwraps the parcel*] Hey!

ERNIE: What is it?

DAD: Looks like a lot of old blue-prints and things. Funny. This anything to do with you?

ERNIE [*innocently*]: No, Dad.

[ATTENDANT *enters with a step-ladder. He places it under the light. A* GIRL LIBRARIAN *who has entered with him steadies the steps.* ATTENDANT *produces a bulb from his pocket and starts to climb the steps*]

ERNIE [*who has been watching him*]: And now, as Captain Williams nears the summit of this, the third highest mountain in the world, never before climbed by man . . .

[*Wind noises start*]

ERNIE: He pauses for a moment through sheer exhaustion . . .

[ATTENDANT *feeling the effects of the wind clings to the ladder for dear life. It sways slightly*]

ATTENDANT [*shouting down to the librarian*]: More slack. I need more slack on the rope . . .

LIBRARIAN [*shouting up to him*]: More slack . . . Are you all right?

ATTENDANT: I—think—I can . . . make it.

LIBRARIAN: Be careful. The rock looks treacherous just above you.

ATTENDANT: It's all right. It's—quite safe—if I . . . just aaaaaahhh! [*He slips and holds on with one hand*]

LADY: Captain! What's happened?

ATTENDANT: Damn it. I think I've broken my leg . . .

LADY: Oh, no.

LIBRARIAN: How are we going to get him down?

[DAD *rises*]

ERNIE: And here comes Major Fraser, ace daredevil mountaineer, to the rescue.

DAD: Give me a number three clambering iron and a hydraulic drill lever, will you? I'm going up.

LIBRARIAN: Oh no, Major.

DAD: It's the only way.

LADY: Don't be a fool, Major.

DAD: Someone's got to go. Give me plenty of line . . . [*He starts to climb*]

LIBRARIAN: Good luck.

LADY: Good luck.

[*A sequence in which* DAD *clambers up the ladder buffeted by the wind*]

DAD: Can you hold on?

ATTENDANT: Not—much—longer.

DAD: Try, man, try. Not much longer . . .

LADY: Keep going, man.

[DAD *reaches the* ATTENDANT. *People cheer. The two men slowly descend the ladder*]

ERNIE: And here comes the gallant Major Fraser, bringing the injured Captain Williams to safety . . .

[DAD *and* ATTENDANT *reach the floor. More cheers and applause from the onlookers. The* ATTENDANT *is still supported by* DAD *with one arm round his neck. General shaking of hands. Wind noise stops*]

ATTENDANT [*coming back to reality, suddenly*]: Hey, hey! What's going on here? [*To* DAD] What do you think you're doing?

DAD: Oh.

ATTENDANT: Let go of me.

DAD: Sorry I—

ATTENDANT: Never known anything like it. This is a public building you know . . .

DAD: Ernie . . .

ERNIE: Yes, Dad.

DAD: Did you start this?

ERNIE [*innocent*]: Me, Dad?

DAD: Now listen, lad—

[*A second* LIBRARIAN *enters screaming*]

2ND LIBRARIAN: Oh, Mr Oats, Mr Oats . . .

ATTENDANT: What's the matter, girl? What's the matter?

2ND LIBRARIAN: There's a man in the Reference Section.

ATTENDANT: Well?

2ND LIBRARIAN: He's dead.

LADY: Dead?

2ND LIBRARIAN: Yes. I think he's been killed. There's a knife sticking in his ribs . . .

[*First* LIBRARIAN *screams.* ATTENDANT *hurries out followed by the others, leaving* ERNIE *and* DAD]

DAD: Ernie!

ERNIE: Sorry, Dad.

[DOCTOR *moves in.* MUM *joins them*]

DOCTOR: Incredible.

DAD: Embarrassing.

DOCTOR: Yes, yes.

[*The scene is now back to where it was at the beginning, with the four in the* DOCTOR'*s room on one side and the waiting room full of patients on the other*]

MUM: Can you do anything, Doctor?

DOCTOR: Mmmm. Not much, I'm afraid.

MUM: No?

DOCTOR: You see, it's not really up to me at all. It's up to you. An interesting case. Very. In my twenty years as a general practitioner I've never heard anything quite like it. You see, this is a classic example of group hallucinations . . .

DAD: Illucinations, yes.

DOCTOR: Starting with your son and finishing with you all being affected . . .

MUM: All?

DOCTOR: All of you. You must understand that all this has happened only in your minds.

DAD: Just a minute. Are you suggesting we're all off our onions?

DOCTOR: Off your . . . ?

DAD: You know. Round the thing. Up the whatsit.

DOCTOR: No . . .

DAD: My missis as well?

DOCTOR: No. No.

DAD: Then watch it.

DOCTOR: I was just explaining . . .

DAD: You don't need. It's Ernie here, that's all. He imagines things and they happen.

DOCTOR: Oh, come now. I can't really accept that.

DAD: Why not?

DOCTOR: It's—impossible. He may *imagine* things—

DAD: He does.

DOCTOR: But they don't *really* happen. They *appear* to, that's all.

DAD: Is that so?

DOCTOR: Of course.

[*Slight pause*]

DAD: Ernie.

ERNIE: Yes, Dad.

DAD: Imagine something. We'll see who's nutty.

ERNIE: What, Dad?

DAD: Anything, son, anything. Just to show the Doctor.

MUM: Nothing nasty, Ernie. Something peaceful . . .

DAD: How about a brass band? I like brass bands.

MUM: Oh dear. Couldn't it be something quieter? Like—a mountain stream or something . . .

DAD: Don't be daft, Ethel. The Doctor doesn't want a waterfall pouring through his surgery. Go on lad. A brass band.

ERNIE: Right, Dad. [*He concentrates*]

[*A pause*]

DOCTOR: Well?

DAD: Give him a chance.

[*A pause*]

MUM: Come on Ernie. [*Pause*] He's usually very good at it, Doctor.

DAD: Come on, lad.

ERNIE: It's difficult, Dad, I can't picture them.

DOCTOR: Yes, well I'm afraid I can't afford any more time just now, Mr and Mrs Fraser. I do have a surgery full of people waiting to see me . . . [*Calls*] Miss Bates! . . . so you will understand I really must get on.

RECEPTIONIST [*enters*]: Yes, Doctor.

DOCTOR: The next patient, please, Miss Bates.

RECEPTIONIST [*going*]: Yes, Doctor.

DOCTOR [*getting up and pacing up and down as he speaks*]: What I suggest we do is, I'll arrange an appointment with a specialist and . . . he'll be able to give you a better diagnosis . . . [*His steps become more and more march like*] than I will. I'm quite sure—that—a—few—sessions—with a trained—psychiatrist—will—be—quite—sufficient—to—put—everything—right—right—left—right—left—left—left—right—left . . .

[*The* DOCTOR *marches to the door of his room, does a smart about turn and marches round his desk. He is followed by the patients from the waiting room, some limping, some marching and all playing, or as if playing, brass instruments*]

L-e-e-e-ft . . . Wheel . . .

[*After a triumphal circuit of the room everyone marches out following the* DOCTOR *who has assumed the rôle of drum major*]

ERNIE [*just before he leaves*]: It looks as though the Doctor suffers from illucinations as well. I hope you don't get 'em. Ta-ta.

[*He marches out jauntily, following the band*]

THE END

The Right Place

DAVID CAMPTON

CAST

ADAM
HUGHIE
PENNY
TUPPENY
BIG BOY
LITTLE GIRL
OLD MAN
1ST WELCOMER
2ND WELCOMER
THE OTHERS

The Right Place

SCENE I: *This play is intended to make the most of the basic magic of theatre—that is, if I say these boards are a garden, then they are a garden, or the top of a mountain, or a sea of treacle: whatever you want. Consequently the action takes place on a bare stage, which means anywhere where it has to take place.*

Enter ADAM. *He is a determined young man. A faraway look in his eyes is balanced by an aggressive thrust to his chin. He knows what he wants, and will not let anyone stop him. He is walking determinedly towards a distant goal.*

He meets HUGHIE, *who is walking in the opposite direction.* HUGHIE *is much more companionable than* ADAM. *He has a ready smile and a friendly manner. He greets* ADAM *with a wave of the hand.*

ADAM *walks straight past* HUGHIE. HUGHIE *turns and hurries after him. The two walk side by side.*

HUGHIE: Going far?

ADAM: Far enough.

HUGHIE: How far is that?

ADAM: Until I get there.

HUGHIE: Where?

ADAM: To the right place.

HUGHIE: Where's that?

ADAM: At the end of the road. It's a very special place.

HUGHIE: What so special about it?

ADAM: Everyone there is a king.

HUGHIE: Everyone?

ADAM: A king. Everyone there does just as he pleases. Everyone there has exactly what he wants. Everyone there is satisfied. Everyone is a king.

HUGHIE: How do you know?

ADAM: In the second place because I was told, and in the first place because I believed. There is such a place. There is. There is.

HUGHIE: I believe you.

ADAM: Why?

HUGHIE: Because it has to be true. You only have to go far enough, and there it is. A golden city. Waiting for you.

ADAM: It won't come to you.

HUGHIE: Can I come with you?

ADAM: The place is there, waiting for anyone. Not many reach it, though. They fall by the wayside.

HUGHIE: Bad luck.

ADAM: It's their own fault. They have to keep going. Keep going. Keep going.

[HUGHIE *pauses to consider.* ADAM *walks away.* HUGHIE *runs after him, and catches him up*]

HUGHIE: Wait for me.

ADAM: I've no time to wait.

HUGHIE: You're not very friendly.

ADAM: I've no time for friends.

HUGHIE: I have.

ADAM: You're not going to the right place.

HUGHIE: I am now.

[*They walk together for a while*]

HUGHIE: My name's Hughie.

ADAM: My name's Adam.

HUGHIE: Pleased to meet you.

[*Still walking, they shake hands*]

HUGHIE: Shall we sing?

ADAM: Singing wastes breath. Never waste anything you may need.

[*Two girls walk towards them. They are sisters*—PENNY *and* TUPPENY. TUPPENY *is bigger than* PENNY]

HUGHIE: There's Penny. [*He waves*] And her sister. [*He waves again*] Tuppeny.

[ADAM *and* HUGHIE *pass the girls*]

PENNY: Hey, wait for us.

TUPPENY: Yes, wait.

[*They walk beside* HUGHIE. TUPPENY *trails a little behind*]

HUGHIE: I can't stop.

PENNY: Why?

TUPPENY: Yes, why?

HUGHIE: Because he won't stop, and I have to keep up with him.

PENNY: Why?

TUPPENY: Yes, why?

HUGHIE: Because he knows where he's going.

PENNY: Don't you?

TUPPENY: Yes, don't you?

HUGHIE: Of course I know where I'm going. I'm going with him. But he knows the way.

PENNY: Is it far?

HUGHIE: You know when you get there. Everyone has everything they want.

TUPPENY: Everyone?

HUGHIE: Everything.

PENNY: Can we come with you?

TUPPENY: Shall we be back in time for tea?

HUGHIE: You may never come back.

TUPPENY: Then I'm not going.

[*She turns to walk back, but* PENNY *catches her hand, and pulls her along with her*]

PENNY: If everybody has what they want, you can have your tea when we get there.

TUPPENY: With iced buns?

PENNY: And trifle.

TUPPENY: Then I'm coming.

[*They walk together for a while*]

TUPPENY: Does he have to walk so fast?

HUGHIE: He's in a hurry. He's the leader.

TUPPENY: I'm in a hurry, too. But I've just had my dinner.

[*As they walk they meet* BIG BOY *and* LITTLE GIRL]

HUGHIE: Hullo, Big Boy. Hullo, Little Girl.

[BIG BOY *and* LITTLE GIRL *turn and keep up with them*]

HUGHIE: We're going to the right place.

PENNY: Where everybody has everything they want.

TUPPENY: With kippers for tea.

PENNY: You said iced buns and trifle.

TUPPENY: I can have kippers, too, can't I?

BIG BOY: You'll be sick.

ADAM: Not in this place. Eat as much as you like, and you're never sick.

PENNY: And it only rains at night when everybody's asleep.

HUGHIE: And everybody is a king.

TUPPENY: And—and . . .

HUGHIE: Come and see for yourself.

LITTLE GIRL: Can we?

HUGHIE: Anyone can come.

[BIG BOY *and* LITTLE GIRL *walk a little way with them. Then* BIG BOY *waves*]

BIG BOY: There are The Others.

ADAM: The Others!

BIG BOY: Everybody else. Can they come?

ADAM: Anyone can come. But I shan't stop for them.

[THE OTHERS *run up chattering, and join the procession*]

ADAM: I shan't stop for anyone or anything. I shan't stop.

THE OTHERS: We shan't stop.

ADAM: I'm going to the right place.

THE OTHERS: We're going to the right place.

ADAM: I shan't turn aside.

THE OTHERS: We shan't turn aside.

ADAM: For anyone or anything. I shan't turn aside or stop. Not until I'm there.

THE OTHERS: Not until we're there.

ADAM: I shan't stop.

THE OTHERS: We shan't stop.

[*An* OLD MAN *with a heavy stick plants himself in front of them*]

OLD MAN: Stop!

[*They all stop*]

ADAM: What do you want?

OLD MAN: I've heard about you.

ADAM: I can't waste time. The only way to get there is to walk straight, without looking to the right or left, without turning aside for anything.

[*He tries to walk past the* OLD MAN, *but the* OLD MAN *moves nimbly from side to side, so that he is always in front of* ADAM, *who cannot pass*]

OLD MAN: I've always wanted to be a king. Only I couldn't find a crown to fit.

ADAM: You shouldn't have stopped.

OLD MAN: Stopped? I never started. I didn't know where to look for the place. Are you sure you know where it is?

ADAM: I wouldn't be going if I weren't sure.

OLD MAN: Then I'll follow you.

ADAM: But you're old. You're like a dried twig.

OLD MAN: I'm fit. Look at my teeth. Not one missing. Count them. Go on. Count them. And three legs. This one. This one. [*Waves his stick*] And this one.

ADAM: You're holding me up.

OLD MAN: I'm not holding anybody up. I'm coming with you.

ADAM: Follow if you like, but I won't wait for you. I won't stop. Not until I get there. I'm going to the right place.

HUGHIE: I'm going to the right place.

PENNY & TUPPENY: We're going to the right place.

THE OTHERS: We're going to the right place, and we won't stop, won't stop, won't stop. We're going to the right place, and we'll never, never, stop.

[*Everyone marches after* ADAM. *The procession is now so long that* ADAM *and* HUGHIE *are out out of sight some time before the* OLD MAN, *who marches stiffly in the rear, swinging his stick*]

THE OTHERS: Never, never, never, never, never, never, never . . .

SCENE 2: *The Meadows. Enter* ADAM *and* HUGHIE. *They are now rather tired, but still making an effort to forge ahead.*

HUGHIE: Don't you ever rest?

ADAM: It's not allowed.

HUGHIE: You'd walk much faster if you rested.

ADAM: I didn't ask for advice.

HUGHIE: You'd go much further after you'd rested.

ADAM [*stumbling*]: What's wrong with my feet?

HUGHIE: They can feel the grass under them. Pause for just a minute.

[ADAM *stops*]

HUGHIE: That's better.

ADAM: One pause leads to another. They join up, stretch out, and keep you from the city.

[*The* OLD MAN *walks briskly up to them*]

OLD MAN: You needn't have waited for me. I can keep up. Not like the others. Look at them. Blisters, corns, and aching legs. Here they come.

[*Everyone else struggles on to the scene. Groaning and complaining, they flop on to the grass*]

PENNY: At last.

TUPPENY: Is it much further?

ADAM: You've only just started.

TUPPENY: It's past tea-time already. And you wouldn't even let me pick blackberries.

BIG BOY: Oh, the grass is soft.

LITTLE GIRL: And there are daisies everywhere.

ADAM: You can't stay here. You mustn't stay.

BIG BOY: The grass is soft.

LITTLE GIRL: And there are buttercups everywhere.

ADAM: If you stay for a minute, you'll stay for ever.

LITTLE GIRL: There are dandelions everywhere.

BIG BOY: And the grass is soft.

ADAM: Soft grass! What does that matter to us? We're not sheep.

BIG BOY: Come and lie on the grass.

ADAM: If you sleep on the grass now, you'll never get there.

BIG BOY: I think I'd rather lie here, and watch the clouds.

ADAM: Then you don't deserve to get there.

LITTLE GIRL: Don't you like flowers?

ADAM: What am I doing here?

HUGHIE: You're resting.

ADAM: I turned aside.

HUGHIE: You needed a rest.

ADAM: If I hadn't turned aside, I'd have been another mile along the road. [*Claps his hands*] Listen to me. Everyone. I'm going on. Now.

[*There is a chorus of grumbles, groans, and complaints*]

ADAM: You can follow if you like. Your feet are your own.

[*The groans increase in volume*]

ADAM: Stay here if you like, but you'll find your own way afterwards.

[*The* OLD MAN *goes around prodding everyone with his stick*]

OLD MAN: Up now. On your feet. Rise and shine. Look at me. [*Marks time*] One-two. One-two. One-two.

[*Reluctantly everyone else, with the exception of* BIG BOY *and* LITTLE GIRL, *get up*]

ADAM: Are you ready?

PENNY: All except Big Boy and his sister.

ADAM: Then I'm off.

[*Resolutely he walks away. The* OLD MAN *marches just behind him*]

OLD MAN: Quick march now. One-two. One-two. One-two. My goodness, you lot should have been in the army. One-two. One-two.

[*Everyone walks off except* HUGHIE *who stands by* BIG BOY *and* LITTLE GIRL]

HUGHIE: You can still catch up if you run.

BIG BOY: Suppose we get to the place, will there be grass like this?

LITTLE GIRL: And buttercups and daisies?

HUGHIE: You'll find everything you want.

BIG BOY: But if the grass there is like this grass, why should we go there? This grass is here.

LITTLE GIRL [*jumping up*]: There's a butterfly. Look. Look! [*She tries to catch it, but fails*] I couldn't catch it.

HUGHIE: In that place you'll be able to catch as many as you want

LITTLE GIRL: But if I catch them, I shan't be able to watch them fly.

BIG BOY [*looking at the others in the distance*]: They're walking very fast. They're almost out of sight.

LITTLE GIRL: But you can catch them if you run.

HUGHIE: Why aren't you coming?

BIG BOY: Because we don't want to waste time.

[HUGHIE *makes a gesture of incomprehension then runs off*]

LITTLE GIRL: He doesn't understand about butterflies.

BIG BOY: Or about grass.

LITTLE GIRL: Look. There's another butterfly.

[*They run off in the opposite direction to the party*]

SCENE 3: *The rocks.* ADAM *enters with the* OLD MAN. *They scramble with difficulty over rocks.*

OLD MAN: All—these—rocks. Are you sure this is the right way?

ADAM: It's the straight way. Straight ahead. Without turning.

OLD MAN: I don't mind rocks. I'm fit. And I've got my stick. But isn't there an easier way?

ADAM: I didn't say the way would be easy. I only said I knew the way. And this is the way.

OLD MAN: Rocks ought not to be left lying about like this. They spoil the view, and somebody might hurt himself. Not me, of course. I've been jumping over rocks all my life. But one of the others. They might break a leg or twist an ankle.

[*Out of sight someone gives a cry*]

OLD MAN: See what I mean?

[ADAM *forges ahead*]

OLD MAN: Aren't you going to stop?

ADAM: I mustn't stop.

OLD MAN: But somebody's hurt. If you were hurt, *we'd* stop.

ADAM: You'd have to. I know the way.

OLD MAN: Oh, go on, then. We'll find somebody else to lead us.

[ADAM *pauses*]

ADAM: For a minute, then. Only for a minute. There isn't time to be sorry for anyone.

[THE OTHERS *come in, forming an excited if unsteady group around* HUGHIE *and* PENNY, *who are carrying* TUPPENY *between them*]

TUPPENY: Don't drop me.

PENNY: You're heavy.

TUPPENY: A pound of me weighs no more than a pound of you.

PENNY: You've never tried carrying yourself.

HUGHIE: Look out for rocks. Don't slip.

ADAM: What happened?

TUPPENY: I found a rock. I slipped.

ADAM: Are you hurt?

TUPPENY: Put me down.

PENNY: You can't stand.

TUPPENY: I can sit.

[*They put her down. She sits rubbing her leg*]

ADAM: Can't you walk?

PENNY: If she could walk, I wouldn't have carried her.

ADAM: *Can* you walk?

TUPPENY: I only twisted something. I'll soon be better.

ADAM: How soon is soon? Until I count to fifty?

TUPPENY: Perhaps not as soon as that.

ADAM: A hundred then?

TUPPENY: A bit longer.

ADAM: Two hundred.

TUPPENY: Try seven hundred and eighty-nine thousand four hundred and sixty-five.

ADAM: How many?

TUPPENY: Or a thousand or two after that. For luck. I might be able to stand after that.

ADAM: I can't wait.

HUGHIE: We can.

ADAM: I knew this would happen. You stop. You feel sorry. And you never get to the right place.

TUPPENY: I can walk as long as I don't use my legs. Look.

[*She tries to stand, but gives a cry and almost falls.* HUGHIE *catches her*]

TUPPENY: There. I can stand—while somebody holds me up.

ADAM: You can't walk fast enough.

HUGHIE: We can't leave her.

ADAM: Then someone must stay with her.

HUGHIE: She'll soon be better. We wouldn't have long to wait.

[TUPPENY *sits down again*]

ADAM: Long enough is too long. I'll count to three. Then I shall start walking again. If you want to stay, you can stay. One.

HUGHIE: You're hard, Adam.

ADAM: You have to be hard to get to the right place. Hard as the rocks. There are so many temptations to hold you back. Two.

HUGHIE: But someone's hurt . . .

ADAM: That's a temptation. Do you think I don't want to stay? I'm sorry for her, and I'd like to help. I'd feel a lot better if I helped. But I have to make a decision. Either I stay or I go on. Confuse your mind, and you forget the way. Are you coming?

HUGHIE: I want to, but . . .

ADAM: Three.

PENNY: I'll stay.

[*She sits next to* TUPPENY]

TUPPENY: No, Penny. You mustn't miss everything you want.

PENNY: If you weren't there, I wouldn't have everything I wanted.

ADAM: If you're coming—come.

[*He walks on*]

THE OTHERS: We're coming. We're coming.

[*They struggle over the rocks after him*]

HUGHIE: I'm sorry.

TUPPENY: Don't worry. You'll make a splendid king.

HUGHIE: Goodbye.

[*He follows the others*]

OLD MAN: Will you need my stick?

TUPPENY: I've got my sister, thank you.

OLD MAN: Oh, yes. Yes. She's better than a stick any day.

[*He follows the others*]

TUPPENY: We came a long way just to go back.

PENNY: Then it's as well you twisted your leg when you did—else we'd have had further to go back.

TUPPENY: We missed our tea.

PENNY: We'll catch up with it when we get home. Can you stand if you lean on me?

[TUPPENY *does so*]

PENNY: With kippers.

TUPPENY: Ah, kippers. With bread and butter. And iced buns afterwards.

PENNY: Now try to walk.

[*Slowly* PENNY *and* TUPPENY *walk in the opposite direction to the others*]

TUPPENY: On second thoughts I'd rather have peaches and cream.

PENNY: Peaches, then. And we'll have kippers tomorrow.

TUPPENY: But iced buns just the same.

PENNY: Iced buns every day.

SCENE 4: The Fog. ADAM, HUGHIE, *the* OLD MAN, *and* THE OTHERS *enter with their arms stretched out in front of them. None of them can see any of the others. They wheel about, sometimes almost touching, sometimes within an inch of colliding, but at the last minute, by chance, always avoiding each other. They call to each other.*

OLD MAN: Fog.

HUGHIE: What is it?

ADAM: It's a fog.

THE OTHERS: Fog. Thick fog. It's a fog.

HUGHIE: I don't like it.

ADAM: I don't like it, either, but I can't stop it.

OLD MAN: I can remember worse fogs than this. I can remember when I couldn't see a hand in front of me. [*He holds up his right hand at arm's length in front of him. He cannot see it. He gropes around with his left hand until he finds his right hand, then pulls his hand towards his face. He still cannot see it*] Oh, much worse than this. But they clear in time. You'll see.

HUGHIE: I can't see.

ADAM: I can't see either.

HUGHIE: Are we all here?

ADAM: Count.

HUGHIE: How can we count if we can't see?

ADAM: Everyone number. Number.

OLD MAN: From the right, number!

[*Four of* THE OTHERS *call out numbers. The others walk off with their hands stretched out*]

ADAM: One.

HUGHIE: Two.

OLD MAN: Three.

THE OTHERS: Four. Five. Six. Seven.

HUGHIE: Is that all? I'm sure there were more of us when we started.

ADAM: Count again.

OLD MAN: Number!

[*One of* THE OTHERS *wanders off*]

ADAM: One.

HUGHIE: Two.

OLD MAN: Three.

THE OTHERS: Four. Five. Six.

[*Pause*]

HUGHIE: Is *that* all?

ONE OF THE OTHERS: That's all.

HUGHIE: That's one less.

ADAM: Are you sure?

HUGHIE: There was one more last time we counted.

ADAM: Then count again.

OLD MAN: Number!

[*One of* THE OTHERS *wanders off*]

ADAM: One.

HUGHIE: Two.

OLD MAN: Three.

OTHERS: Four. Five.

[*Pause*]

HUGHIE: Again.

ONE OF THE OTHERS: Five.

HUGHIE: Did you say five?

THE OTHER: Of course I said five.

HUGHIE: Then who said six?

THE OTHER: Nobody said six.

HUGHIE: But why didn't anybody say six?

THE OTHER: Because there are only five of us.

HUGHIE: There were six. Somebody said six.

OLD MAN: You said nobody said six.

HUGHIE: Somebody said six last time.

ADAM: They said five this time.

HUGHIE: Then we've lost another.

ADAM: Another?

HUGHIE: Every time we count, we're one short.

ADAM: Count again.

HUGHIE: No. Don't count again, or there'll soon be none of us left.

ADAM: Don't be silly. How can we lose anybody? There's nowhere to go. Nowhere.

OLD MAN: Number.

[*One of* THE OTHERS *wanders off*]

ADAM: One.

HUGHIE: Two.

OLD MAN: Three.

THE OTHER: Four.

[*Pause*]

HUGHIE: Again.

THE OTHER: Four.

HUGHIE: I told you so. We're down to four. What's happening to us?

OLD MAN: A light. I can see a light. Shining over there.

ADAM: It's shining in the wrong direction.

HUGHIE: Yes, it's lamplight. It's firelight.

ADAM: Don't look at it. It's dangerous. It will lead you from the path.

HUGHIE: All I can see is fog and the light. The fog is cold and grey. The light is warm and bright.

ADAM: Follow me. Follow me.

HUGHIE: But I can't see you.

ADAM: Hold my hand.

HUGHIE: I can't see your hands.

ADAM: Here they are.

[*They grope around, and eventually* HUGHIE *finds* ADAM's *hand*]

HUGHIE: Ah!

ADAM: Everybody hold hands.

OLD MAN: Here's mine.

HUGHIE: Where?

OLD MAN: Here. Here.

HUGHIE [*grasping his hand*]: Got you.

ADAM: Are we all here?

OLD MAN: I'm here.

HUGHIE: I'm here.

ADAM: And I'm here.

HUGHIE: Who else?

OLD MAN: There's nobody else.

HUGHIE: But there's only three of us left.

OLD MAN: We're lucky. There might have been none of us.

HUGHIE: Are you sure you know the way?

ADAM: It's this way. This way. I can see the place in my mind. It's this way.

[*Holding hands, they go out. The last of* THE OTHERS *is standing on his own*]

THE OTHER: The light. I'm coming. I can see the light.

[THE OTHER *goes out in the opposite direction*]

SCENE 5: *The River. Enter* ADAM, *followed by* HUGHIE *and the* OLD MAN. HUGHIE *is pulling the* OLD MAN, *who is looking back.*

HUGHIE: Come on, Old Man. What's so interesting back there? I can only see men working.

OLD MAN: I used to work once. Then somebody said I was too old to work. I wasn't, of course. But somebody said I was, so I had to stop working.

[ADAM *stops at the river. He looks up and down and across it*]

ADAM: A river. I hadn't expected a river.

HUGHIE: We'd better look for a place to cross.

ADAM: We must cross here.

HUGHIE: But there isn't a bridge.

ADAM: The road goes straight. It turns neither to the right nor to the left. It goes straight to the city—through forests, over mountains, across rivers. That's how we know it's the right road. It's a straight road. It goes on and on.

HUGHIE: But we can't cross here. We haven't got a boat.

OLD MAN: They're cutting corn back there. Swish. Swish.

ADAM: What did you say?

OLD MAN: Swish. Swish. It's the old way. I told them I used to cut corn that way. Swish swish. So they asked me to join them.

ADAM: What are you talking about?

OLD MAN: They were short of men, and they were in a hurry. They wanted to cut the corn before the rains came. They asked me to work with them. Swish. Swish.

HUGHIE: But you're going to the right place.

OLD MAN: That's what I told them. So I couldn't stay to work with them. It's a pity really, because I was good at it. Swish. Swish.

ADAM: We shall have to go into the river.

HUGHIE: But we'll get wet.

ADAM: We can dry ourselves on the other side.

HUGHIE: It's wide.

ADAM: The further we get from this side, the nearer we shall be to the other.

HUGHIE: He's an old man.

OLD MAN: Don't you talk about me, boy. I was crossing rivers before you were born. Who'll get their feet wet first, eh? Follow me.

[*They walk into the river*]

OLD MAN: What were you worrying about, eh? It only comes up to my knees. This isn't a river. It's no more than a trickle.

[*But as the water rises to their waists, they find walking more difficult*]

HUGHIE: It's—it's—it's—cold. And it's up to my waist.

ADAM: It's bound to get deeper yet. We're nowhere near the middle.

OLD MAN: Forward, lads. Forward.

[*They press on, but move even more slowly as the water rises higher*]

HUGHIE: It flows faster here. I can hardly push against the current.

ADAM: Forward. Forward. We're not far from the middle now.

[*He goes forward, but the* OLD MAN *starts to slip back.* HUGHIE *glances behind, and sees him*]

HUGHIE: Old man. Old man. Come on.

OLD MAN: I can't. This river's too much for me.

[HUGHIE *splashes back as* ADAM *presses forward and out of sight*]

OLD MAN: Don't wait for me. I'm a fool who doesn't know how old he is.

HUGHIE: Let me help you.

OLD MAN: You go on. Go on, I said. Go on.

[HUGHIE *supports the* OLD MAN *as they make their way back to the bank*]

OLD MAN: I told you to go on. If you turn back now, you'll never get to the right place. Don't waste time.

HUGHIE: Don't waste your breath. You may need it.

[*Panting, they reach the shallows*]

HUGHIE: Here we are. Back among the bullrushes. And here's the bank. Give me your hand. [*He pulls the* OLD MAN *on to the bank, then they both sit down*] Dry ground. Oh, it feels good.

OLD MAN: You could have been at the other side of the river by now. Why didn't you go on?

HUGHIE: If I had, you'd have floated away. [*He looks across the river*] There's Adam. [*He jumps up and down, and waves*] He just crawled out on the other side. Hi, Adam! Here we are! We're safe! . . . He didn't look back. Perhaps he didn't hear me.

OLD MAN: You should have let me float away. I'm no use to anyone.

HUGHIE: Oh yes, you are.

OLD MAN: I'm too old for anything.

HUGHIE: You can still cut corn. Swish. Swish. And the men back there want help. We can help them. Swish. Swish.

OLD MAN: That's right. Swish. Swish.

HUGHIE: Come on. [*He walks with the* OLD MAN. *At the last minute* HUGHIE *turns*] He looks very small now. Just a black speck. Well, he started alone. Now he's finishing alone. [*He goes out with the* OLD MAN]

SCENE 6: *The Right Place. Enter* ADAM.

ADAM: The road goes straight. Through the forest. Over the mountain. Across the desert. Straight on. Straight on. [*He is almost exhausted. He staggers and almost falls*]

ADAM [*stretching out his arms*]: It must be. It must be. With great shining towers. There. Here. Only a few more steps away. Only—a few—more . . . [*He falls*]

ADAM: Here. Here.

[*He tries to get up, but does not quite manage it. He falls flat again, and this time lies still. Two* WELCOMERS *enter and run to him. Each looks like one of* THE OTHERS. *Each has a satchel*]

1ST WELCOMER: Did you see him first, or did I?

2ND WELCOMER: Did you want to see him first?

1ST WELCOMER: No, but I thought you might have wanted to.

2ND WELCOMER: Then let's have seen him first together.

[*They examine* ADAM. *The* 1ST WELCOMER *heaves him up to a sitting position. The* 2ND WELCOMER *looks at his feet*]

2ND WELCOMER: Look at his feet. He must have walked a very long way.

1ST WELCOMER: Well, he's here now. Are his eyes open?

2ND WELCOMER: I believe they are.

ADAM: Water.

1ST WELCOMER: Certainly.

[*He takes a large bottle from his satchel and puts it to* ADAM'*s mouth.* ADAM *drinks*]

ADAM: That was good. I feel much better now. [*He stands up*]

1ST WELCOMER: Of course you do.

2ND WELCOMER: Isn't it funny how they always ask for water?

ADAM: I didn't expect you'd have lemonade.

1ST WELCOMER: Try this. [*Offers the bottle again*]

ADAM: But that's the same bottle.

1ST WELCOMER: Try it.

[ADAM *drinks*]

ADAM: It's lemonade!

1ST WELCOMER: Made with real lemons. Was it cold enough for you? Or would you rather have it fizzy?

ADAM: And if I'd asked for champagne?

1ST WELCOMER [*offering the bottle*]: Try it.

ADAM: Then I found the right place at last.

2ND WELCOMER: This is where you wanted, isn't it?

ADAM: Who are you?

2ND WELCOMER: We are the Welcomers for today.

ADAM: Don't I remember you?

1ST WELCOMER: That's up to you. Do you want to?

[*The* 2ND WELCOMER *takes a crown from his satchel and hands it to* ADAM]

2ND WELCOMER: Your crown, sire.

[*The* WELCOMERS *bow*]

1ST WELCOMER: King Adam the seven hundred and sixty-fourth.

BOTH WELCOMERS: The King is alive. Long live the King.

[*The* WELCOMERS *salute smartly*]

2ND WELCOMER: You were expecting it, weren't you?

1ST WELCOMER: We all do.

ADAM: Where are your crowns?

2ND WELCOMER: We don't bother much for everyday. They get in the way so. You'll wear yours for a while, of course. Just to get the feeling.

1ST WELCOMER: We've arranged a triumphant procession for you, too. Bands and flags and girls strewing flowers.

ADAM: Thank you.

2ND WELCOMER: It's what you expected, isn't it?

ADAM: It's what I hoped for.

1ST WELCOMER: Oh, then. You'll get it.

2ND WELCOMER [*calling*]: To me, everyone. To me. Procession starting from here.

[*A crowd gathers to welcome* ADAM. *They look like* THE OTHERS. *A girl curtsies and presents a bouquet to* ADAM. *She is* LITTLE GIRL *and is accompanied by* BIG BOY. PENNY *and* TUPPENY *curtsey as they pass.* TUPPENY *is eating an enormous ice-cream.* ADAM *is about to speak to them, but changes his mind. The* OLD MAN *enters, carrying a drum*]

OLD MAN: Get fell in there. One-two. One-two. One-two. Can't wait about all day. I've got to get back to work.

ADAM: But that's . . .

1ST WELCOMER: Standard Bearer in front. Where is the Standard Bearer?

[HUGHIE *runs up with a flag*]

HUGHIE: Here.

ADAM: Hughie!

HUGHIE: I'm glad you got here in the end.

ADAM: But—you were left behind.

HUGHIE: Yes, that was a pity. You took so much longer.

ADAM: But how did you get here? And him—and her—and him—and her?

HUGHIE: We stopped long enough to see what was around us. You took longer to here get because you were trying so hard. But you're here now. Are you ready?

[ADAM *nods*]

HUGHIE: Is everybody ready? Banners, bells, bands, flowers, fireworks, cheers and a twenty-one gun salute? All right then. Forward march.

[*Bands play, crowds cheer, bells peal, and guns boom as the procession moves off*]

THE END

Arthur

DAVID CREGAN

CAST

ARTHUR

AUNT ALICE

CAPTAIN OF THE FIRE BRIGADE

CHIEF FIREMAN

FIRE BRIGADE

FREDERICK

DENISE

MAYOR

LADY POLICE INSPECTOR

GERTRUDE

LADY POLICE FORCE

SCOUT COMMISSIONER

OTTER PATROL

SCOUT MESSENGER ONE

SCOUT MESSENGER TWO

Arthur

SCENE I: *Someone throws cups and saucers on the floor off-stage.*

AUNT ALICE [*off*]: Arthur!

[*Enter* ARTHUR]

ARTHUR [*to the audience*]: I hate Aunt Alice. [*To* AUNT ALICE] If you treat me like a little boy, there's nothing for it but to fight. I'm twenty-one and I *will* go out with girls.

[*Enter* AUNT ALICE *holding a large teapot*]

AUNT ALICE: This is rebellion.

ARTHUR: Yes.

AUNT ALICE: You're fighting for your independence.

ARTHUR: Yes.

AUNT ALICE: Thank heavens. At last you're growing up. [*She hands him the teapot*] You left this.

ARTHUR: It's rather large.

AUNT ALICE: Have the courage of your convictions. If you're going to smash the cups and saucers you must feel able to smash the pot as well. [*He throws it off-stage. There is a smash*] Splendid. Now the furniture. [*She goes off*]

ARTHUR: I've made my point, Aunt Alice.

AUNT ALICE [*off*]: There's more to this than making points. [*She enters with a large axe*] Start on the dining-room table.

ARTHUR: I can't do that. I've had so many pleasant meals there.

AUNT ALICE: Don't be sentimental, Arthur. Out with everything, root and branch. That's the secret of good revolution. [*She goes out, leaving him holding the axe*]

ARTHUR [*to the audience*]: I only want to be like other boys
Who, at my age, have stopped playing with toys.
I want to take out girls and feel able to relax.
Aunt Alice always takes things too far.
For heaven's sake, an axe!

[*Enter* AUNT ALICE *with a flaming torch*]

AUNT ALICE: Give me liberty or give me death! The staircase is the place to start a house burning, I believe.

ARTHUR: But it's *your* house, Aunt Alice.

AUNT ALICE: Of course. You've had a dreadful childhood, your adolescence has been misery, you've never had a chance to form your own opinions, and I'm entirely to blame.

ARTHUR: That's more or less true.

AUNT ALICE: Then blot it out. Here's the flaming brand of freedom. [*She places the torch in* ARTHUR'S *free hand*]

ARTHUR: This is madness.

[AUNT ALICE *pushes him off*]

AUNT ALICE: 'If you can lose your head when all about you are keeping theirs and blaming it on you—'

ARTHUR [*as he disappears*]: I wish it was yesterday.

SCENE 2: *A firebell rings. Enter the* FIRE BRIGADE, *and the* CAPTAIN.

CAPTAIN: Fire Brigade, from the left, number!

[*They do,* CHIEF FIREMAN *being No 1*]

Right. [*He rubs his hands*] A fire at last. As Captain of the first computer-operated fire brigade in the country, I expect you to put this out efficiently and return within the hour, faces blackened and sweat dripping from your chins. Understood?

FIRE BRIGADE: Yessir!

CAPTAIN: We haven't had a fire since the introduction of the smokeless zone, so don't spoil it.

FIRE BRIGADE: Nosir!

CAPTAIN: Lots of heartbreaking interviews, and somebody please choke nearly to death.

CHIEF: Frederick.

CAPTAIN: I shall be with the computer, but I'll be out there with you in spirit. Remember the eyes of the Mayor and Corporation will be on you to see if you were worth the cost of modernising, so everything depends on you.

FIRE BRIGADE: We are the noble Fire Brigade!
Yohoho and chemical foam!
Going to rescue a poor old maid,
Risking our lives to save her home!

[*The* CAPTAIN *leaves them, as, under the direction of the* CHIEF FIREMAN, *they rush round the stage collecting equipment and prepare to put out the fire by aiming their hoses off stage*]

CHIEF: Are you ready! Take aim, steady—

[*A sudden shower of pots and pans hurls on to the stage and drives them back*]

Hullo? Is anybody there?

AUNT ALICE [*off*]: Mind your own business.

CHIEF: It *is* our business.

A FIREMAN: Yohoho and chemical foam.

AUNT ALICE [*off*]: This is a family matter. It has nothing to do with you.

CHIEF: All fires have something to do with us.

ARTHUR [*coming in*]: It's very kind of you to come.

AUNT ALICE [*also coming, though very angry*]: It is not! It's an interference with the rights of private individuals. Go away.

CHIEF: Someone may be dying in there.

[*The* FIRE BRIGADE *agree with him*]

AUNT ALICE: We're all quite safe, so don't make that excuse. It's part of my nephew's development, throwing off the chains of adult tyranny. Please take your gang of busybodies somewhere else before I send for the police.

CHIEF: But your home and your possessions! Look at them!

AUNT ALICE: Arthur is a very spirited boy. I'm proud of him.

CHIEF [*in anguish and frustration*]: But we're the Fire Brigade! We exist to put out fires!

FIRE BRIGADE [*anxiously*]: We are the noble Fire Brigade! Yohoho and Chemical foam!

Going to rescue a poor old maid,
Risking our lives to save her home!

AUNT ALICE: If you haven't left in thirty seconds, I will prosecute you for trespassing. This is *our* fire and we don't want any bureaucratic interference.

ARTHUR [*interrupting*]: Since they're here, Aunt Alice, I think you might let them have a try.

FIRE BRIGADE [*hopefully*]: We are the noble Fire Brigade! Yohoho and—

AUNT ALICE [*silencing them*]: They're civil servants! And those silly hats will make them bald before they're thirty.

FIRE BRIGADE: No, we want to fight the fire, etc., etc.

AUNT ALICE [*loudly*]: Discipline!

[*They are silent*]

Now go.

CHIEF: This is very irregular.

AUNT ALICE: Most things are.

CHIEF: And you haven't heard the last of it.

[*He goes out followed by the muttering* FIRE BRIGADE]

AUNT ALICE: Don't weaken, Arthur. You're doing very nicely. [*She goes out*]

SCENE 3: ARTHUR *is standing alone.*

ARTHUR [*to the audience*]: When I was a little boy
I used to sit and dream
Of being a much bigger boy
With permission to eat ice cream.
When I was a bigger boy
I used to wonder why
Nobody would let me have
Two helpings of apple pie,
Ever.
Now I am a boy no more
And grown to man's estate,
I want to sit down and weep.

[*Enter* DENISE]

DENISE: Whatever are you doing, Arthur?

ARTHUR: I'm in rebellion against the older generation.

DENISE: I suppose you can see your aunt's house is on fire?

ARTHUR: I did that.

DENISE: Did you? Whatever will they say at work?

ARTHUR: Will you go to the pictures with me?

DENISE: Well, I don't know, Arthur. You're rather a dangerous person.

ARTHUR: Are you fascinated by me, Denise?

DENISE: Well, I don't know, Arthur. You aren't very usual, are you?

ARTHUR: I'm fascinated by you.

DENISE: Are you? Well, I don't quite know what to say.

ARTHUR: I'm fascinated by many girls.

DENISE: Well, I don't know, really, what to think. Has your aunt been burnt to death?

ARTHUR: Shall I kiss you passionately?

DENISE: Well, I don't know. I don't think we've known each other long enough.

ARTHUR: We've been to school together since we were five, I've done your homework for you, you've shared your sweets with me, we've worked in the same office for three years. How much longer must I know you before I can kiss you passionately?

DENISE: The thing is, Arthur, it doesn't seem right, not while your aunt's burning to death in there.

ARTHUR: Who cares about Aunt Alice? Hoho! I'm free of the wicked old Gorgon!

DENISE: Ooooh! Well!

ARTHUR: So what about it, Denise? A passionate kiss while my home burns to the ground?

DENISE: Well, to be quite frank, Arthur, I'd rather not. It seems a bit funny. Unless you call the Fire Brigade, of course.

ARTHUR: I've sent the Fire Brigade away.

DENISE: You what?

ARTHUR: If you don't fancy kissing, Denise, say so. Don't make excuses.

DENISE: To be quite honest, Arthur, I think you must be peculiar. I do, really. So if you don't mind, I'll be on my way.

[*She goes*]

ARTHUR [*calling*]: Denise!
[*to audience*] Now I am a boy no more
And grown to man's estate,
There's nothing more to dream about.
I've got here,
And somehow I'm starting on the wrong foot.

[*He goes off*]

SCENE 4: *Enter the* MAYOR *and the* CAPTAIN.

MAYOR: What d'you mean, rights of the individual? Have you never heard of law and order?

CAPTAIN: She said it was *her* house, so—

MAYOR: Suppose I burnt down the Town Hall?

CAPTAIN: It isn't yours to burn down.

MAYOR: Of course it isn't. It's part of England. And her house is part of England. She's set fire to the mother country. You realise that?

CAPTAIN: It's *her* part of it.

MAYOR: *Her* part? Who's Mayor of this town?

CAPTAIN: You are.

MAYOR: Exactly. So her house is mine. All for one and one for all.

CAPTAIN: I don't quite follow.

MAYOR: You're dangerously liberal in your views, Captain. Where were you when it happened?

CAPTAIN: Somebody has to sit by the computer.

MAYOR: Oh yes. The computer. The most expensive fire-fighting equipment in the country and in two years it has rescued three hundred and fifty-one cats. Explain *that* to the ratepayers.

CAPTAIN: There just haven't been the fires.

MAYOR: Until today. And today there were newspaper reporters, press photographers television camera-men, and radio commentators.

CAPTAIN [*crestfallen*]: I know.

MAYOR: And you were sitting by the computer in case some-one stole it.

CAPTAIN: Someone has to read what it says.

MAYOR: You have a wife and children, Captain?

CAPTAIN: Yes, sir.

MAYOR: You don't want them to go hungry?

CAPTAIN: No, sir.

MAYOR: We'll hear no more about the rights of individuals, then, will we?

CAPTAIN: No, sir.

MAYOR: We'll hear no more of playing with computers while the town bursts into flames?

CAPTAIN: No, sir.

MAYOR: I want that woman arrested under the laws of arson.

CAPTAIN: By the Fire Brigade?

MAYOR: Don't be ludicrous. By the female police. [*Wagging his finger*] I'm warning you, I'm warning everyone. This town is going to be cleaned up.

[*They go off*]

SCENE 5: *Enter a group of* POLICEWOMEN *and a female* POLICE INSPECTOR.

INSPECTOR: From the left, number!

[*They do so*]

Female Police Force, stand at—ease!

[*They do so*]

Right, girls. Our first criminal. Are you afraid?

POLICEWOMEN: No, ma'am.

INSPECTOR: Splendid. Courage, mes braves. Chins high, shoulders back, and we don't want any feeble noddies whimpering about the milk of human kindness. Just because she's an old lady who's lost everything in the world, there's no excuse for anyone to feel sorry. Is that clear?

POLICEWOMEN: Yes, ma'am.

INSPECTOR: This woman is a dangerous influence on the youth of this town. She is cunning, she is strong. We will employ Tactic D on her. You remember Tactic D?

POLICEWOMEN: Yes, ma'am.

INSPECTOR: Very well, then. Atten—tion!

[*They obey*]

POLICEWOMEN: We are the noble women's police!

INSPECTOR: Yohoho and Chanel No 5.

POLICEWOMEN: Helping to keep the public peace,
Helping our citizens all to thrive.

INSPECTOR [*putting herself where she will lead them off*]: Female Police Force, left—turn! Quick—march! Left, right, left, right.

[*They go off*]

SCENE 6: *A tent is brought on. Out of it come* ARTHUR *and* AUNT ALICE.

AUNT ALICE: Well, well. This is what you've brought me to, Arthur. A tent in what was once the drawing-room fireplace. What a scourge of your enemies you are.

ARTHUR: No, Aunt Alice. It's no use pretending. I'd like to feel I was a really wicked man, but you did all this, not me.

AUNT ALICE: Don't annoy me, Arthur. Why aren't you taking a girl to the pictures, or spooning down some quiet lane? It's a lovely night.

ARTHUR: No-one goes spooning with a man who burns down houses. They think he's mad.

AUNT ALICE: You're too good for them. You know that.

ARTHUR: It makes me lonely.

AUNT ALICE: Loneliness is a habit. You must break it.

ARTHUR: I don't find you very understanding, Aunt Alice. If I'm lonely, I don't see how I can stop it.

AUNT ALICE: Take somebody by storm, Arthur. Bowl them over. Use that splendid brain of yours.

ARTHUR: Splendid brain! You know I've lost my job.

AUNT ALICE: I always said you were . . .

ARTHUR: Too good for it. Perhaps.

AUNT ALICE: I don't believe you're happy. That's your trouble.

ARTHUR: I don't believe I am.

AUNT ALICE: Don't be sarcastic with me. If you're not happy you must put it right.

ARTHUR: How?

AUNT ALICE: *I* don't know. You're free of my influence now. Oh Arthur, it's so disappointing to have your house burnt down in a blaze of revolutionary zeal and then to find that the hero won't take the credit for it. You must live up to your image.

ARTHUR: If you don't mind I'll take a little walk and try to think clearly. [*He sets off round the stage*]

AUNT ALICE [*to the audience*]: Oh!
It's quite maddening, growing old,
Having to assist the young.
You're either too timid or else too bold,
And you can't just hold your tongue.
To repress all one's notions
Would lead to psychological explosions.
One would go mad. [*She sits outside her tent*]

SCENE 7: *There is a giggle off-stage, near where* ARTHUR *has arrived.*

ARTHUR [*looking off*]: Denise? Is that a member of the Fire Brigade I see kissing you passionately?

FREDERICK [*off*]: Yes.

[DENISE *and* FREDERICK *come on*]

I'm a member of the Fire Brigade!
Yohoho.
My name is Frederick.

DENISE: Doesn't he look smart. Put your helmet on, Frederick.

[*He does*]

ARTHUR: He bowls you over, I suppose.

DENISE: Completely. The only thing is, Arthur, you've about ruined him.

ARTHUR: *I* have?

DENISE: More or less broken his spirit, not letting him put your fire out.

ARTHUR: I'm sorry.

DENISE: Being sorry's no good.

FREDERICK: The Captain might lose his computer, too.

DENISE: You've brought misery to everyone, in fact. And it's not as though you *are* anyone. Poor ruined Frederick, it's a shame.

ARTHUR: He's got *you*, Denise. He's got his nice uniform.

DENISE: It's his vocation we're talking about. You wouldn't know about that sort of thing, I suppose. He's lost without a fire to put out.

ARTHUR: I've lost *my* job as well.

DENISE: You weren't a fireman. You were only an accounting clerk. Frederick feels a call, you see, it's not just a job with him.

ARTHUR: He should go somewhere else where they have fires, then. Vesuvius.

FREDERICK: I don't fancy living abroad.

DENISE: So like I said, you haven't exactly helped, have you?

ARTHUR: I can only say I'm sorry.

DENISE: That's all you ever seem to say. Come along, Frederick, let's leave him. He's a deviationist.

[*They go*]

ARTHUR [*calling after them*]: If it's a vocation he should go wherever it calls him! That's what a vocation is! Uncomfortable! [*To himself*] Like me. Except, as she says, I haven't a vocation. And yet— My splendid brain! You have revealed a possible course for my future. Suddenly I see the clouds begin to part. Behold the new Arthur Parsons!

SCENE 8: ARTHUR *walks round the stage back to his aunt.*

ARTHUR [*as he goes*]: This is the noble Arthur Parsons!
Yohoho and great renown!
See on his shoulders how he fastens
All the troubles of this town. [*He arrives at the tent*]
Aunt Alice, you must now accept the consequences of letting me grow up. You're to be my vocation.

AUNT ALICE: I'm a dead end, Arthur. Aim your sights higher.

ARTHUR: You've no choice in this, Alice Parsons. You've involved yourself with me and now, miserable, homeless wretch that you are, you must obey me.

AUNT ALICE: Arthur?

ARTHUR: You've upset the authorities, and unless they're more than human they'll want their revenge. It's my duty to save you from that. It's also the first step in my career. Who knows what heights it will lead me to?

AUNT ALICE: Is this you speaking, Arthur?

INSPECTOR [*off and in a loud whisper*]: Tactic D!

ARTHUR: There!

POLICEWOMEN [*off and in a whisper*]: Tactic D!

[*The* POLICEWOMEN *and the* INSPECTOR, *whispering their chorus, crawl in on their tummies.* ARTHUR *goes over to a group of them, kneels down, and speaks to* POLICEWOMAN GERTRUDE CROSBIE. *He talks in a low voice.* THE POLICEWOMEN *talk in whispers when they reply*]

ARTHUR: Good evening. I expect you're here for some reason.

GERTRUDE [*whispers*]: To make an arrest.

ARTHUR: Of my aunt?

GERTRUDE: I'm not permitted to reveal that.

ARTHUR: But I'm right, aren't I?

GERTRUDE: Yes.

[ARTHUR *sits beside her*]

ARTHUR: Would you like to go to the pictures?

GERTRUDE: I'm on duty.

A POLICEWOMAN: You're talking to the enemy, Gertrude.

GERTRUDE: He started it. I've got to reply.

ARTHUR [*to policewoman*]: Would *you* like to go to the pictures?

A POLICEWOMAN: Of all the cheek!

ARTHUR: Well, would you?

GERTRUDE: You asked me first.

ARTHUR: Then answer.

GERTRUDE: Quite honestly, yes, I would.

INSPECTOR [*in loud whisper, like the others*]: Policewoman Crosbie, what are you doing?

ARTHUR [*aloud and standing up*]: She's making a date with me to go to the pictures. I'm infiltrating the forces of reaction.

AUNT ALICE: I'm so glad! Why's she lying on her tummy?

INSPECTOR [*leaping up*]: It's Tactic D! [*She blows her whistle*] Right girls, truncheons ready!

[*They all stand up, truncheons ready*]

INSPECTOR: Miss Alice Parsons, formerly of 22, The Grove, we arrest you in the name of the law for committing a breach of the peace by allowing your house to burn down. I should warn you that—

ARTHUR: Stop.

INSPECTOR: Is this rowdyism?

ARTHUR: You're arresting the wrong woman.

AUNT ALICE: Don't fuss, Arthur. You go to the pictures and let them arrest me.

ARTHUR: This Miss Parsons still lives at 22, The Grove. There's no formerly about it.

INSPECTOR: Nonsense. 22, The Grove burnt down this morning.

ARTHUR: If you'd come in by the front gate you'd have seen the number 22 still written on it. If you'd followed the garden path up the front steps, through what's left of the front door, you'd have come to this tent where Miss Alice Parsons still lives. The word 'formerly' in your charge obviously means you should arrest someone else.

POLICEWOMEN: Bravo, hooray, etc, etc. [*They clap*]

ARTHUR: *Now* I'll go to the pictures. You're free from any threats, Aunt Alice. [*To* INSPECTOR] Isn't that so?

INSPECTOR: You realise you're making yourself very unpopular with the authorities, young man?

ARTHUR: Facts are facts. You've got yours wrong, I'm afraid.

AUNT ALICE [*impressed*]: Arthur! You've got a mind like a steel trap.

A POLICEWOMAN: Absolutely. A steel trap.

[*Murmurs of agreement from the others*]

INSPECTOR: Girls! I suspect some of you of being unreliable.

AUNT ALICE: I think you should know I'm a third Dan Black Belt at Judo.

INSPECTOR: The Mayor will not be pleased with any of this. [*Placing herself where she can lead the* POLICEWOMEN *off*] Female Police Force! Fall—in! Left—turn! Quick—march! Left, right, left, right, etc.

[*She marches off alone. The others have not reacted. They slide off backwards, gazing at* ARTHUR *in admiration during the following*]

AUNT ALICE: I've underrated you. You *are* a hero after all.

ARTHUR: Let's not be hasty. First things first. [*He links arms with* GERTRUDE *and they move away*]

POLICEWOMEN [*in chorus*]: Good night Gertrude.

GERTRUDE: Lucky me.

[*All go off except* AUNT ALICE]

AUNT ALICE [*to the audience*]: It's so much easier when the chickens leave the nest

At least it's possible to rest. [*She smiles happily at the audience and goes into the tent*]

SCENE 9: *Enter* FREDERICK.

FREDERICK [*to the audience*]: Hohoho. It's all very well saying go to Vesuvius. You can't put out a volcano. [*To the others off-stage*] Men!

[*Enter the* FIRE BRIGADE]

This is a spontaneous meeting. Our interests have been threatened. After today it's clear society has no use for us, so we must demand out rights. More fires!

CHIEF: This is inflammatory talk, Frederick.

FREDERICK: We have a calling. This community doesn't allow us the freedom to exercise our talents.

ALL: Hear, hear!

FREDERICK: So we must act!

CHIEF: You aren't suggesting we *light* fires?

FREDERICK: No. Work to rule. That is, in future we shall put out fires whether anyone wants us to or not. And when we're called out to rescue pets, or unlock doors, we must insist on emptying our chemical foam containers into the houses concerned, and hacking down a minimum of three doors with our specially provided firemen's axes. And when the computer calls us out to non-existent fires, we must insist on putting them out nevertheless.

ALL: Hear, hear!

FREDERICK: I think that's reasonable.

CHIEF: I'll put it to the Captain.

A FIREMAN: We don't want to lose our uniforms, after all. We are loved for our uniforms.

ALL: Hear, hear!

CHIEF: I understand your case, and will speak to the authorities. Meanwhile disperse and say nothing. These are troubled times.

[*They all walk off nonchalantly except for one man*]

A FIREMAN [*to the audience*]: You too will have a job one day,
You may have one already.
If you like it, then you'll stay,
And hope it'll be steady.
But if the world moves on without you,
Leaving your job unheeded,
You'll be like us, the Fire Brigade,
Who found that buildings had been made
Too safe, and you will be dismayed
To find you are not needed.

And men not needed, I have heard it said,
Would be much happier, friends, if they were dead. [*He goes off*]

SCENE 10: *Enter the* MAYOR, *the* CAPTAIN, *the* INSPECTOR, *and the* BOY SCOUT COMMISSIONER.

MAYOR: I trust you all heard that? I trust everyone realises we're facing revolution? I've no doubt there are similar feelings among the Policewomen, aren't there, Inspector?

INSPECTOR: I'm afraid Arthur Parsons is turning into a cult figure among my girls, Mr Mayor.

MAYOR: It's difficult to believe that a man with a wife and family to support, and a woman with instalments to pay on her car, should put their jobs in such danger as you have done. Arthur Parsons will have to go.

CAPTAIN: You aren't going to use force?

MAYOR: Of course not. I'm a reasonable man, and reason makes it plain that this tent is not No. 22, The Grove. What is it, then, you may ask?

OTHERS: Yes.

MAYOR: It's an eyesore, and so is not to be tolerated. Now, who would live in an eyesore?

OTHERS: Who?

MAYOR: A gypsy. Therefore there's a gypsy living here, and as you know, gypsies are not allowed.

INSPECTOR: Alice Parsons is living here.

MAYOR: Then Alice Parsons is a gypsy, and must be removed. Humanely. That's why the Commissioner for Boy Scouts is with us. It's Bob-A-Job Week and there's a Five Bob Job going here if he wants it.

COMMISSIONER: We're a voluntary organisation, Mr Mayor. You can't force us.

MAYOR: A Ten Bob Job.

COMMISSIONER: Thank you. The movement will be grateful, I'm sure. [*Calling off*] Otters! [*He puts his hand on his head, the Scout sign for 'Come here'*]

[*Enter a patrol of* BOY SCOUTS]

SCOUTS: We are the noble Otter Patrol!
Yohoho and a running bowline!
Helping the Mayor to get out of a hole,
Stopping the status quo from rollin'.

MAYOR [*taking out a wad of ten-shilling notes which he hands round to the* BOY SCOUTS]: Dear lads, young England as I like to call you, we are faced with an untidy situation. Now, untidiness, as you know, leads to uncleanliness, filth, squalor, and the collapse of law and order. For you boys, who have done so much to keep Britain tidy in the past, here is a great challenge. This tent contains an agent of disruption we can't allow in our community. You will remove her and her tent, without disturbing her, to the town dust heap. Society will never forget you. Don't think of this money as pay. It's a present from a grateful old Mayor, who sees in you the hope of the future. All right, Commissioner.

COMMISSIONER: Otters! To the dust heap.

[*They push off the tent singing quietly the Scout song 'As our trek cart goes rolling along'. The* MAYOR *and the* COMMISSIONER *follow them*]

CAPTAIN: Are you quite happy about this, Gladys?

INSPECTOR: People must behave properly. That's their contract with society.

CAPTAIN: Is it?

INSPECTOR: Of course. Take my advice, go back to your computer, and forget about it.

CAPTAIN: I must say, machines are easier than people.

[*They go out*]

SCENE II: *Enter* ARTHUR *and* GERTRUDE.

ARTHUR: What a lovely evening, Gertrude. Are you fascinated by me?

GERTRUDE: Yes.

ARTHUR: That's the reason you let me kiss you passionately when you'd only known me for an hour.

GERTRUDE: You know everything, Arthur. One day you'll be a great man.

ARTHUR: That's quite probable. The difficulty is deciding what sort of great man to be.

GERTRUDE: Time will reveal everything.

ARTHUR: The first thing I want is to go out with more girls.

GERTRUDE: Aren't I the only girl for you?

ARTHUR: I ought to have wider experience. After all, you *are* a Policewoman.

GERTRUDE: I think I'm more fascinated by you than you are by me.

ARTHUR: Oh no, I'm sure not.

GERTRUDE: Then will you marry me, before you become too grand to think about me?

ARTHUR: If I'm to be a great man, I can't become enslaved again, Gertrude.

GERTRUDE: I want to help you, Arthur, not enslave you.

ARTHUR: That's what they all say. [*He notices the tent is missing*] Where's she gone? Someone's taken away Aunt Alice. Policewoman Crosbie, blow your whistle!

GERTRUDE [*desperately*]: Arthur, marry me!

ARTHUR: Blow your whistle!

GERTRUDE: Oh! It's over before it started! [*She blows her whistle*]

ARTHUR: All men are some time masters of their fates.
The fault, dear Crosbie, lies not in our stars
But in ourselves that we are underlings. [*He kneels*]
Aunt Alice, you have made a man of me.
Now it's my duty to see that you are free.

SCENE 12: *Enter the* FIRE BRIGADE, *the* POLICEWOMEN, *and the* INSPECTOR.

INSPECTOR: Policewoman Crosbie, can you explain yourself?

ARTHUR: Someone has removed my aunt while we were at the pictures. Who was it, please?

INSPECTOR: Arthur Parsons, have you taken the liberty of blowing Policewoman Crosbie's whistle?

FREDERICK: Troublemaker.

GERTRUDE: I blew it myself.

ARTHUR: Who has removed Alice Parsons?

[*Silence*]

It was you, Frederick, wasn't it? Revenge for letting the fire burn.

FREDERICK: I don't know anything about it.

GERTRUDE: Did any of you girls do it?

A FIREMAN: She set a bad example.

A POLICEWOMAN: Oh you firemen! Why don't you do something positive with your lives?

INSPECTOR: That'll do.

A POLICEWOMAN [*muttering*]: Well.

ARTHUR: Shall I have to ask the Watch Committee, ma'am, why an old woman disappeared from beneath your eyes?

INSPECTOR: You're growing rather too big for your very ill-mannered boots, young man.

POLICEWOMEN: 2, 4, 6, 8,
Who do we appreciate?
A-R-T-H-U-R. Arthur! [*They clap*]

INSPECTOR: There. A personality cult. How unreliable the modern girl is.

ARTHUR: A public investigation, ma'am? Misappropriation of elderly relatives?

INSPECTOR [*to audience*]: A cleft stick. [*To* ARTHUR] One day you'll know what it means to have your loyalties divided.

ARTHUR [*very grand*]: Who stole Alice Parsons?

INSPECTOR: The Boy Scouts.

FREDERICK: Strike action. A volunteer body being used to do the work of professionals.

[FIRE BRIGADE *take off their helmets. The fire-bell rings*]

Ignore that, all of you.

INSPECTOR: The Mayor had your aunt designated a gypsy and she's been taken to the town dust heap.

ARTHUR: You allowed it?

INSPECTOR: Try not to think harshly of an Inspector of Police with twelve instalments to pay on her car.

ARTHUR: I begin to see what greatness means. I must have my aunt back at once.

[*Enter the* CAPTAIN *very excited*]

CAPTAIN [*ecstatic*]: Fire! The second in twenty-four hours! Oh that I should live to see the day!

FREDERICK: We're striking, Captain.

CAPTAIN [*so happy that he hasn't heard*]: The whole town's ablaze, or else the computer's gone mad. It started at the Mayor's house, and now it's moving down the High Street. [*To the* FIRE BRIGADE] Your second chance, lads. Seize it, for all our sakes.

FREDERICK [*distressed*]: But we're on strike.

CAPTAIN: On strike? This is the whole town, Frederick. There'll never be another fire if we don't save some of it for next time.

CHIEF: Fire Brigade! Helmets—on!

[*They put them on*]

FREDERICK [*as they do so*]: Well, it *is* a vocation. We aren't like ordinary workers.

ARTHUR: Instinct tells me that Aunt Alice is safe.

CAPTAIN: Ready? Follow—me! Left-right, left-right, etc.

[*They trot off after the* CAPTAIN. *A* BOY SCOUT *rushes in*]

SCOUT: News. Most alarming and amazing news. [*He kneels at* ARTHUR'S *feet*]

ARTHUR: A messenger, I think.

SCOUT: No sooner had we taken your aunt down the High Street than she woke and started to complain. Within minutes, using her knowledge of Judo, she had laid out the Scout Commissioner and half of Otter Patrol. All the rest, save only I, fled for safety. Then using a Karate stroke, she chopped a large branch from a tree, lit it from a nearby street light, and standing before the Mayor's house, swore most horribly.

ARTHUR: What did she say?

SCOUT: A Scout is clean in thought, word and deed. I didn't listen.

ARTHUR: It's good to see ideals in the young. Reward him.

[*Enter another* BOY SCOUT]

SCOUT: Further news, more alarming and amazing still. [*He kneels in front of* ARTHUR]

ARTHUR: A second messenger.

GERTRUDE: They recognise you as a born leader, Arthur. They all come to you.

ARTHUR: I noticed that. Very pleasing.

GERTRUDE [*joining the other* POLICEWOMEN]: It's all over between us. He's grown too great for humble Gertrude Crosbie.

SCOUT: The Mayor, having arranged for Miss Alice Parsons to be thrown away, retired to bed as usual in the front bedroom of his house. Woken by the awful curses of Miss Parsons, now to his amazement on his front lawn, he peered out of his window just as the Fire Brigade, on their automatic ladders, needlessly summoned by their computer, released the chemical foam from the nozzles of their hosepipes, according to their new practice of working to rule. Soaked, the Mayor fled, pursued by your aunt. Because she still held the flaming branch, the computer-operated machinery followed too, and the Fire Brigade, working still to rule, insisted on trying to extinguish him.

ARTHUR: Where is he now?

SCOUT: In the Town Hall, switching off the electricity supply.

[*Enter* AUNT ALICE, *carrying the remains of her branch*]

AUNT ALICE [*furious and grand*]: I have suffered remarkable indignities.

ARTHUR: My dear aunt, so I hear. Send for the Commissioner of Scouts.

[*The* BOY SCOUTS *run off*]

And arrest the Mayor.

[*The* POLICEWOMEN *run off*]

Aunt Alice, my poor old thing, I'm afraid it's been more than you bargained for, letting me grow up. However, we can't reverse the tide of things, and I am very nearly very great. Everything will be restored to you at the expense of His Worship the Mayor. And if he can't afford it, the rate-payers will.

AUNT ALICE: Bleed him white, Arthur. Have him rebuild 22, The Grove.

[*Enter the* BOY SCOUTS, *and the* FIRE BRIGADE, *using hose-pipes like guns to make the* MAYOR *keep his hands up. He is soaking wet. The* CAPTAIN *is with him*]

CAPTAIN: But Your Worship, you miss the point. The fact is that clearly our machinery works extremely well and clearly our Fire Brigade *is* the most efficient in the country after all.

MAYOR: Why didn't you turn it off when you saw how efficient it was being?

CAPTAIN: You said I mustn't sit by the computer any more.

ARTHUR: Mr Mayor. I should warn you all has been revealed, or nearly, and you are disgraced.

MAYOR [*to audience*]: The trouble with living in this country is, you aren't allowed to shoot your political opponents. I have done my duty as I saw it.

[*Enter the* SCOUT COMMISSIONER *in the custody of the* POLICEWOMEN]

COMMISSIONER: Mine was not to reason why,
Mine was but to do or die.
Before you say anything against me, let me explain that this is Bob-A-Job week, and when the Mayor offered me a bribe—

ALL: Shame!

COMMISSIONER: I yielded for the good of the cause.

ALL: Shame.

COMMISSIONER: Yes. I suppose so. I must be a very wicked Scout Commissioner. I hand in my resignation at once.

ARTHUR: And Mr Mayor?

MAYOR: I did my best for the community.

ALL: Never.

MAYOR: I did what I thought was best for the community.

ALL: Never.

[*He takes off his chain of office*]

MAYOR: I seem to have been a very wicked Mayor, though I doubt if you'll get a better, and I hand my resignation in at once.

ARTHUR: Now here's a situation. We have no Mayor. Tch. Tch.

AUNT ALICE: We look round for a new Mayor, and where do our eyes rest? The answer, fellow citizens, is plain. Our eyes rest on Arthur.

ARTHUR: So they do.

ALL: 2, 4, 6, 8,
Who do we appreciate?
Arthur!

[*Silence. Then* ARTHUR, *wearing the chain of office, steps forward to speak to the audience*]

ARTHUR: This little tale began with a rebellion,
With casting off my youth, you may recall,
With growing up to man's estate,
A thing, you will appreciate,
That happens willy nilly to us all.

I wanted to go out with girls, remember,
But girls, they didn't want to go with me.
Well now the story's over
You would think I'd be in clover,
But I'm not. Just watch a moment and you'll see.

[*Kneeling*] Gertrude Crosbie, I think now I'm in a position to support a wife and family. I can hold my head up in the world with pride and say, I am a man of substance. Will you marry me?

GERTRUDE: No, Mr Mayor. I'm very honoured, but I could never keep up with someone as great as you.

ARTHUR: True. You're doing the sensible thing, Gertrude.

[DENISE *rushes on*]

DENISE: I could keep up with you. I think you're absolutely smashing, Arthur, and so does Mum.

FREDERICK: Denise!

DENISE: Oh, hullo, Frederick. I don't know that you're quite respectable any more, leading strikes and everything.

FREDERICK: What about my vocation?

DENISE: Well, I don't know. You haven't got the class, have you?

ARTHUR: Denise, you are the last person in the world I could marry now. Yesterday morning, yes, but today I've tasted greatness, and the taste of you would be very nasty in comparison.

DENISE: Well, thanks for nothing.

AUNT ALICE: Arthur has a high destiny. We must allow him to fulfil it.

ARTHUR [*to audience*]: So there we are:
I've come far
And may go further still.
But please, consider if you will,
Those of you who think good has triumphed over bad,
What sort of influence has been had
On my character?

A FIREMAN: He means that sooner or later
He will probably become a dictator.

ARTHUR: You see? And I still haven't gone out with any girls.
Not really.

A POLICEWOMAN: In fact he sacrificed true love for his career,
Quite clearly.

ARTHUR: So think on that. And in the meantime, goodnight.

[*Everybody bows*]

THE END

The Crickets Sing

BEVERLEY CROSS

CAST

ORLANDO NOKES (a Dramatic Author)
A LANDLADY (of 'The Mermaid')
CORPORAL JAGGER
COLONEL FITCH
LUKE
DRUMMER POTTS
(of the City Trained Bands)
DR CHILLINGWORTH (Dean of Christ Church)
KING CHARLES THE FIRST
QUEEN HENRIETTA MARIA
PURITANS, ROUNDHEAD SOLDIERS,
ROYALIST LORDS AND LADIES . . .

The Crickets Sing

SCENE I: *A winter wind howls. An inn sign—depicting a buxom mermaid—swings and creaks . . . We are in the City of London in the year 1642; in an inn known as 'The Mermaid'. Along the length of a table, some half dozen men sit drinking ale. They are all dressed in black. No one speaks, no one smiles. The* LANDLADY *stands watching them. She yawns . . . Then enter the wild figure of* ORLANDO NOKES—*a Dramatic Author. He clutches a large pile of manuscript pages; and in his hair and on his clothes are wisps of straw.*

ORLANDO: What a day! I'm frozen to the bones! A pot of mulled ale, if you please, hostess. And the same for any gentleman who cares to join me!

[*The customers all look down at the table*]

. . . Oh, very well. Please yourselves. But this is a triumphant occasion for me, you understand. It is finished! After three years—finished at last! [*He thumps the thick wad of manuscript*]

LANDLADY [*giving him a pot of steaming ale*]: What's finished?

ORLANDO: My play! My tragedy! My masterpiece! *The Life and Death of Ethelred the Unready* in five acts, sixteen scenes, and an epilogue—including six new songs and a depiction of his massacre of the Danes in 992 . . . My finest work!

LANDLADY: A 'play', did you say?

ORLANDO: Yes. A play. *My* play. *Mine* . . . A play by Orlando Nokes—at your service.

[*He bows with a flourish. All the men in black—all save one—quickly put down their pots of ale and hurry away*]

But what's the matter? Have I said something wrong?

LANDLADY: How long did you say you've been writing this . . . [*she whispers*] 'play'?

ORLANDO [*whispering*]: Three years.

LANDLADY: And where?

ORLANDO: I've been in the country—living like a hermit in a little woodcutter's hut in Enfield Chace, out beyond Hertford. I travelled in on a hay cart this morning.

LANDLADY: Ah! So you've not heard then?

ORLANDO: 'Heard' what?

LANDLADY: About the war.

ORLANDO: What war?

LANDLADY: This one.

ORLANDO: This one? What one? Where?

LANDLADY: Everywhere. The King is fighting the Parliament.

ORLANDO: Whatever for?

LANDLADY: Oh, don't ask me. I don't understand politics. But you must understand that here, in London, you're on the side of the Parliament; leastways, you'd better be!

ORLANDO: Then where's the King?

LANDLADY: In Oxford. Three weeks ago there was a great battle at a place called Edgehill—near Warwick.

ORLANDO: Who won?

LANDLADY: Nobody's quite sure. The King says he won, the Parliament says we've won. You pays your taxes and you takes your choice . . . But one thing's sure . . .

ORLANDO: Yes?

LANDLADY: Don't you go bragging about your play.

ORLANDO: Why ever not?

LANDLADY: The Parliament don't approve of plays.

ORLANDO: But the theatres . . . ?

LANDLADY: All shut—by order.

ORLANDO: Shut?

LANDLADY: And all the actors fled to France.

ORLANDO: Fled?

LANDLADY: And last week they caught a playwright.

ORLANDO: Caught?

LANDLADY: A nice young fellow—just like you . . . you know what they did?

ORLANDO: No.

LANDLADY: They nailed him by the ears to a pillory.

ORLANDO: Oh, my goodness!

LANDLADY: Said he was guilty of doing the Devil's work.

Said no decent people should see, hear, or even read plays—for they are temptations inspired by Lucifer.

ORLANDO: But my play's very serious, and extremely historical . . . Nothing wicked in it—it's about Ethelred the Unready . . .

LANDLADY: Please. I don't want to hear anything about it. It wouldn't be good for business.

ORLANDO: But what am I going to do? This is my life's work—well, three years of it anyway. It's really too much. A Civil War, of all things! How could they do this to me! . . . I tell you what, though, I refuse to be thwarted. My play is very fine, very important. It *must* be performed. And if London doesn't want it, then I shall take it where it will be appreciated . . . I shall take it to Oxford! To the King himself!

LANDLADY: Sssh . . . ! Do be cautious, Mr Nokes.

ORLANDO: A fig for caution, madam! Leave caution to the politicians and the soldiers . . . I happen to be an Artist! [*He turns to leave. But his way is blocked by the one remaining customer,* JAGGER]

JAGGER: One moment, Mr Nokes.

ORLANDO: Out of my way.

JAGGER: One moment, I said. One moment, I mean. [*He draws back his black cloak to reach for a large pistol. Under the cloak he is wearing a soldier's scarlet leather jerkin, and his belt is stuffed with weapons*]

ORLANDO: I see. Forgive me, my friend. I was simply blustering to hide my disappointment. You surely sympathise. You are, as I can see, a man of the world . . .

JAGGER: I'm Corporal Jagger of the City Trained Band.

ORLANDO: A soldier!

JAGGER: A corporal. And I'll trouble you to come along with me.

ORLANDO: But I'm going to Oxford.

JAGGER: Oh no, you're not.

ORLANDO: I'm not?

JAGGER: No. You're coming with me.

ORLANDO: May I ask 'where'?

JAGGER: You may.

ORLANDO: . . . Where?

JAGGER: The Tower of London . . . So look sharp now. And quick march! Left, left, left, right, left . . . !

[*He flourishes his pistol. Nervously, trying to get into step,* ORLANDO *obeys. He exits, followed by* JAGGER. *The* LANDLADY *is left holding the wad of manuscript*]

LANDLADY: . . . Poor young man . . . such nice, pink ears too . . . [*She looks at the manuscript*] . . . He didn't pay for his drink, but this will keep the kitchen fire going till Christmas . . . It's going to be a long, hard winter . . . [*She clears the table of pots and exits*]

SCENE 2: *The sign of 'The Mermaid' is replaced by the banner of Parliament—a quartered flag with the Cross of St. George in the first and fourth quarters, the Cross of St. Andrew in the second, and the Irish Harp in the third. Drum rolls and a trumpet call, and we are in The Tower of London. Enter a soldier bearing the personal standard of* COLONEL FITCH *of the City Trained Band—a mailed arm holding a sword over the legend 'For Ye Cause of Law, My Sword I draw' . . . Enter the fierce* COLONEL FITCH, *followed by a sly, shifty-looking fellow*—EZEKIAL LUKE.

COLONEL: Anything to report, Luke?

LUKE: Corporal Jagger made an arrest this morning, Colonel Fitch.

COLONEL: Splendid.

LUKE: He apprehended one Orlando Nokes—a playwright and, I believe, a former actor.

COLONEL: Very good. I always enjoy dealing with this sort. They're such cowards, you know—always squeal and shriek.

LUKE: With this case, Colonel, perhaps we shouldn't be in too much of a hurry to rush him to Tower Hill.

COLONEL: Why ever not? He writes plays, doesn't he? That's good enough for me. He's guilty. Send him to the pillory . . . Not like you, Luke, to be squeamish. Off your food, are you?

LUKE: I was thinking of our little plan, Colonel. The Oxford plot . . .

COLONEL: Which one was that? You think up so many. You should have been a playwright! Ha, ha; what!

[LUKE *does not laugh*]

LUKE: It seems this Nokes has written a play. Jagger heard him swear to take it to the King in Oxford.

COLONEL: So?

LUKE: We've been looking for some sort of cover to get us into Oxford, to bring us near the King . . . This fellow might be the very man.

COLONEL: You think so?

LUKE: We could try. Should our plot succeed, it would mean the end of the war at one blow.

COLONEL: And a handsome reward from a grateful Parliament.

LUKE: And certain promotion . . . Colonel . . .

COLONEL: Ah! Now you're talking, Luke! *General* Fitch . . . Yes, I should like that . . . Send in the prisoner!

LUKE: Send in the prisoner!

[*Enter* ORLANDO, *guarded by* CORPORAL JAGGER]

ORLANDO: Good afternoon. Distinctly chilly for the time of year, don't you think?

COLONEL: Silence, Nokes.

ORLANDO: Of course, Captain.

COLONEL: I am a Colonel.

ORLANDO: Frightfully sorry. Then I'm not very knowledgeable about the military. I serve the Arts—or, rather, I did!

LUKE: You write plays?

ORLANDO: Not any more. No. I gave all that up—this morning.

LUKE: Then you must take it up again—this afternoon.

ORLANDO: But what about my ears?

LUKE: They'll not be touched. Not if you do what we ask.

ORLANDO: Oh, rest assured, gentlemen—I'll do anything you want. You see, I'm a dreadful coward.

COLONEL: Told you so, Luke. They're all the same—no backbone.

ORLANDO: None at all. You're absolutely right, Captain . . . er, I mean, *Colonel.*

LUKE: As well as writing plays, do you also act?

ORLANDO: I used to—before I retired into the country to write my tragedy, that is.

[*The* COLONEL *and* LUKE *exchange sinister smiles*]

LUKE: Then there just might be a way out for you, Nokes.

ORLANDO: I do hope so.

LUKE: A way by which you might avoid your lawful and deserved punishment.

ORLANDO: Anything, sir. I'll do anything.

LUKE: Excellent. We want you to go to Oxford and perform a play before the King.

ORLANDO: *You* want *me*? . . . [*He whispers*] . . . A *play*?

LUKE: You will be rendering a great service to the Parliament.

ORLANDO: I will?

LUKE: And at no possible danger to yourself.

ORLANDO: Well, I'm all for that!

COLONEL: And if you succeed, I'll see that you get a safe passage to France.

ORLANDO: Succeed? But of course I'll succeed. I'm a very gòod actor. Why, my performance as Mark Antony was highly praised . . . 'Friends, Romans, Countrymen! Lend me your ears! . . .'

COLONEL: Silence, Nokes. Or you'll be lending me *your* ears—and you might not get them back!

ORLANDO: I do apologise. An unfortunate quotation—in the circumstances. Very unfortunate.

LUKE: Quite. The Colonel was not referring to your personal success but to the success of the *real* purpose of your visit to Oxford.

ORLANDO: Real purpose?

LUKE: You will lead a company of players to Oxford and perform before the King. But while you are presenting your play, another drama will be enacted in another part of Oxford.

ORLANDO: It will?

LUKE: The King, the Queen, everyone of rank will be in Christ Church Hall watching *you,* Nokes. But I—I, Ezekiel Luke . . .

ORLANDO: Ezekiel . . . what a charming name!

LUKE: Thank you. I shall be in New Inn Hall. For there, Nokes, there is the secret weapon that keeps the King's armies in the field.

ORLANDO: I'm not very good on weapons . . .

COLONEL: Luke is getting carried away again, Nokes. He means money. New Inn Hall is now a Mint. That's where the King is melting down all the silver cups, goblets, pots, dishes, spoons and baubles that used to decorate the tables of all the Oxford colleges.

LUKE: He's melting them down and turning them into money.

COLONEL: Money to pay his soldiers . . .

LUKE: Money to buy swords and pikes . . .

COLONEL: Money for horses and hay . . .

LUKE: Gunpowder and cannon-balls . . .

COLONEL: Without that money, the King is helpless.

LUKE: He'll be forced to surrender.

COLONEL: We'll have won! The war will be over!

ORLANDO: Hurrah! . . . Sorry—I was carried away for a moment. What a splendid plot—I wish I'd written a play about that, I really do. Only one thing . . .

LUKE: Well?

ORLANDO: What about the last Act? How do you get the money *out* of Oxford?

LUKE: You bring it with you—after you've performed your play.

ORLANDO: Do I? . . . But *how*?

LUKE: In the chest.

ORLANDO: What chest?

LUKE: I was coming to that. You see, you'll have to perform a play in which a chest forms part of the plot. A big chest. A big, roomy sort of chest . . . If they've seen a chest in the play, then they'll naturally accept it—they won't bother to search it . . . Now, what plays in your repertoire require a chest?

ORLANDO: There's a chest in *Henry the Fifth*—when the French King sends King Hal a box full of tennis balls by way of an insult . . . [*He strikes a suitable pose*]

'When we have matched our rackets to these balls,
We will in France, by God's grace, play a set
Shall strike his father's crown into the hazard . . .'

. . . But it's not really my part, you know. Terribly noisy and hearty. I prefer more sensitive roles.

LUKE: What about that play where the fat old man hides in a basket full of washing and gets thrown into the Thames?

ORLANDO: *The Merry Wives of Windsor* . . . No. Sir John Falstaff's not in my line . . . Ah! What about *Cymbeline*?

COLONEL: Never heard of it.

ORLANDO: I'm not surprised. Dreadful old nonsense, don't you know. Shakespeare fiddled about with it after Beaumont and Fletcher gave up. But there's a good villain's part for me—Iachimo. And there *is* a trunk. A big, roomy trunk. It has to be, because Iachimo has to hide in it.

[*The* COLONEL *again looks to* LUKE. LUKE *nods*]

COLONEL [*briskly*]: Then *Cymbeline* will do very well. You will leave for Oxford tonight. In a week's time, you will play before the King . . . Good luck, Nokes.

ORLANDO: Thank you, Colonel . . . Just one, small question.

COLONEL: Yes?

ORLANDO: A tiny, unimportant detail . . .

COLONEL: Out with it, man.

ORLANDO: Well, I can't perform a play on my own—talented as I am . . . What am I going to use for actors?

COLONEL: Yes. I see the problem . . . We hadn't thought of that, had *you*, Luke?

LUKE: Not exactly . . .

COLONEL: There are no actors left in London. You'll have to make do, as I do, with volunteers. Corporal Jagger—parade the Guard.

JAGGER: Sir! . . . [*Shouting close to* ORLANDO'S *ear*] . . . Fall in the Guard!

[ORLANDO *winces. A drum-beat is heard. Enter* DRUMMER POTTS *followed by a platoon of* SOLDIERS. *They halt in a line before* COLONEL FITCH]

COLONEL: There you are, Nokes. A platoon of volunteers. Fine-looking lot, aren't they?

ORLANDO: Fine. But a trifle *big*—perhaps it's only their boots . . . And what about Imogen?

COLONEL: Who?

ORLANDO: The Princess—the heroine of the story.

COLONEL: Use the smallest. Drummer Potts there.

ORLANDO: Him?

COLONEL: He'll be all right if you smarten him up a bit. After all, he *is* a musician.

[ORLANDO *examines* DRUMMER POTTS]

ORLANDO: Can you sing, boy?

POTTS: I can sing 'ymns, sir.

ORLANDO: *Hymns.*

POTTS: *Hymns and psalms.*

ORLANDO: Well, there's a nice little song in *Cymbeline* . . . Try the first two lines. After me, if you please . . . [*He sings*] . . . 'Hark! hark! the lark at Heaven's gate sings . . .'

POTTS: ' 'Ark! 'ark! the lark at 'eaven's gate sings.'

ORLANDO: *H*ark! *h*ark!

POTTS: *H*ark! *h*ark!

ORLANDO: That's better . . . Well, Colonel Fitch. If there's really nothing better . . .

COLONEL: Nothing.

ORLANDO: It'll be a battle . . .

COLONEL: Then just make sure you *win.*

ORLANDO: I'll try. I can make no promises—but I'll try.

COLONEL: Splendid. I like a man of spirit. And just to make sure you *keep* trying, Corporal Jagger will be right beside you. And Luke will be right behind you . . . So you're now in command, Nokes. Off you go, and the best of luck.

ORLANDO: Thank you. Most kind . . . Now then gentlemen, after me, if you please . . . [*He sings*]
Hark! hark! the lark at Heaven's gate sings,
And Phoebus' gins arise,
His steeds to water at those springs
On chaliced flowers that lies;

[*The* SOLDIERS *begin to join in.* DRUMMER POTTS *thumps out the beat on his side-drum*]

ORLANDO & SOLDIERS: And winking Mary-buds begin
To ope their golden eyes:
With every thing that pretty is,
My lady sweet, arise:
Arise! arise! . . .

ORLANDO: Gentlemen, by the left, quick march!
And you there—in the middle—don't slouch.
You're not in the Army now . . . You're an *Actor*!

ORLANDO & SOLDIERS [*as they march out*]: Arise! Arise!
My lady sweet arise:
Arise! arise . . .!

[*They march out with a fine swagger.* LUKE *salutes the* COLONEL, *winks knowingly, then slinks out in the rear of the platoon . . . The singing fades. The* COLONEL *and his standard-bearer exit together in the opposite direction*]

SCENE 3: *The banner of Parliament is replaced by the arms of Christ Church College, Oxford—The Cardinal's Hat. We are now in Christ Church Hall . . . Enter a weary* ORLANDO. *He sighs and tries to brush down his cloak and polish the mud off his boots. Enter the ancient and pedantic figure of* DR CHILLINGWORTH, *the Dean of the College.*

CHILLINGWORTH: Are you the actor?

ORLANDO: Orlando Nokes, at your service.

CHILLING: I am Dr Chillingworth, Dean of this College of

Christ Church, and, for the moment, His Majesty's Master of the Revels. The King and Queen will hear your play tonight—after supper.

ORLANDO [*looking round cautiously*]: Never mind the play, Doctor. You're the very man I must speak with . . .

CHILLING: What's that? You must not mumble, Mr Nokes. I am a little deaf . . .

ORLANDO: I must speak with you—a matter of great importance and urgency.

CHILLING: I've been Dean of this College for forty years.

ORLANDO: My congratulations, Dean. But if you'd only listen for a few minutes . . .

CHILLING: Forty years this last Michaelmas. Why, I remember the end of our beloved Queen Elizabeth as if it was yesterday . . .

ORLANDO: Most interesting, Doctor. Fascinating . . . But please listen to me. I am in the grip of ruthless men . . .

CHILLING: I had lodgings in New Inn Hall Lane . . . A clean, sunny room and as much ale as I could drink—all for fourpence a week. Ah! Those were the days, Mr Bokes.

ORLANDO: Nokes! The name is Nokes. But New Inn Hall, that's the very place they're planning to rob. The silver, Dean . . . The Silver and the Money!

CHILLING: Yes. Money used to mean something in those days. Fourpence wouldn't go far these days, Mr Bokes.

ORLANDO: Nor will you if you don't listen! . . . Please, Dean, New Inn Hall . . . [*shouting*] . . . New Inn Hall!

CHILLING: Yes, you're in the Hall . . . Magnificent, isn't it? Cardinal Wolsey planned it, you know.

ORLANDO: Not *this* Hall . . . Another Hall! . . . *New* . . .

[LUKE *suddenly appears—smirking*]

LUKE: You were saying, Orlando?

ORLANDO [*laughing nervously*]: About the Hall, Ezekiel, old friend. The dear Dean was talking about Cardinal Wolsey, weren't you, Dean!

CHILLING: You must speak up, you know, young man. And you, an Actor . . . Now, in my day . . .

LUKE: Who is this buffoon?

ORLANDO: He's the Dean, *and* the Master of the Revels.

LUKE: Is the performance all arranged then?

CHILLING: . . . many players used to come here . . . I recall one very excellent piece about Julius Caesar . . .

ORLANDO: All arranged. We play before the King and Queen tonight—after supper.

LUKE: Where?

ORLANDO: Here in the Hall.

CHILLING: Yes, you're in the Hall . . . Cardinal Wolsey planned it . . .

ORLANDO: Oh dear, oh dear! What a trying week! What a ghastly day! . . . I shall never be able to give my best tonight.

LUKE: You had better . . .

CHILLING: . . . Of course, he never saw the finished buildings . . .

ORLANDO: Who's he talking about now?

LUKE: I don't know. Get rid of him.

CHILLING: I shall be sixty-two next Easter . . .

ORLANDO: Remarkable. You don't look a day over ninety.

CHILLING [*sharply*]: I heard that, young man.

ORLANDO: Nineteen. I meant nineteen, didn't I, Ezekiel?

LUKE: Get rid of him!

ORLANDO: Yes. Well, thank you so much, Dean. You've been most kind. But we must get on. Rehearsals and all that . . . We'll have a long talk—later.

[*Enter* JAGGER *and the Platoon—now disguised as Players. They drag on a large trunk*]

ORLANDO: Over there with the trunk . . . Yes. That will do very well . . . Come along, everybody, places, please. We haven't got all day . . . William! You're still slouching! . . . Potts, stop chewing. I won't tell you again! [*In his enthusiasm, he bumps into* DR CHILLINGWORTH]. . . . So sorry. Thank you for everything, but now I must have time and privacy to rehearse.

LUKE: This way, Doctor. [*He takes* CHILLINGWORTH'*s arm, and steers him out of the Hall*]

CHILLING [*as he goes*]: These young people. No respect nowadays . . . When I was a boy, I was taught to be polite . . . And I only wanted to watch. I'm very fond of '*Julius Caesar*' . . .

[*He exits.* LUKE *returns*]

LUKE: You weren't trying to give us away, were you, Nokes?

ORLANDO: What a foolish suggestion! After a whole week of agony trying to teach these clumsy oafs how to speak, how to walk . . . do you seriously think I'd throw all this effort away? You've a suspicious nature, Ezekiel. I'm disappointed in you.

LUKE: Well, just in case; you, Corporal Jagger, keep your eye on him. Don't let him out of your sight for a second.

JAGGER: Very good, sir.

LUKE: I'm off to spy out the approach to New Inn Hall . . . [*He taps the trunk*] . . . See you rehearse well, Orlando. We don't want the King to get bored, do we? [*He chuckles nastily, then slinks off*]

ORLANDO: A coarse sense of humour, that fellow. No feeling for the Arts . . . And you're not much better, Potts! Stop chewing! You're supposed to be a Princess. And a Princess never chews.

POTTS: Please, Mr Nokes, sir. I'm not chewing, sir. I'm shaking. And my mouth is all dry.

ORLANDO: Ah! Then, I apologise, Potts. You are experiencing stage-fright. That's very good. There's hope for you yet. At last, you are displaying a capacity for emotion . . . I shall make an Artiste of you yet!

POTTS: But if I feel like this, sir, now, sir—what will it be like tonight when I have to do it? What will it be like at nine o'clock?

ORLANDO: At nine o'clock tonight, Potts my boy, you will not be alone.

POTTS: I won't, sir?

ORLANDO: No, Potts. Like you, we shall all be—every man Jack of us—absolutely, desperately, horribly *terrified*! . . . Come. Let us go prepare our costumes. After you, Corporal Jagger . . . Would that the night were come!

[*The Platoon of Players troop out. The trunk holds the stage . . . A bell tolls nine*]

SCENE 4: *Trumpets. Enter a Royalist soldier bearing the King's personal standard—the Royal Arms of England supported by the Lion and the Unicorn beneath the legend 'Give Caesar his Due' and over the motto 'Dieu et mon Droit' . . .* KING CHARLES THE FIRST, QUEEN HENRIETTA MARIA, *and several Royalist* LORDS *and* LADIES *appear. They group themselves—watching the play . . . A fanfare . . . The* KING *and* QUEEN *lead a round of applause . . . Music . . . Enter* DRUMMER POTTS—*now disguised as* IMOGEN. *He lies down on a couch by the trunk, and begins to read a book by the light of a candle. Enter a soldier* [WILLIAM] *dressed as a* NURSE.

POTTS: Who's there? My woman, Helen?

WILLIAM: Please you, madam.

POTTS: What hour is it?

WILLIAM: Almost midnight, madam.

POTTS: I have read three hours then; mine eyes are weak;
Fold down the leaf where I have left; to bed:
Take not away the taper, leave it burning,
And if thou canst awake by four o'clock,
I prithee, call me. Sleep has seized me wholly.

[*The* NURSE *exits*]

To your protection I commend me, Gods!
From fairies and the tempters of the night
Guard me, beseech ye!

[IMOGEN *sleeps.* IACHIMO (ORLANDO *in a villain's make-up*) *comes from the trunk*]

ORLANDO: The crickets sing, and man's o'erlaboured sense
Repairs itself by rest . . . Imogen,
How bravely thou becom'st thy bed! Fresh lily!
And whiter than the sheets! That I might touch!
But kiss: one kiss! Rubies unparagon'd,
How dearly they do't! 'Tis her breathing that
Perfumes the chamber thus . . . But my design,
To note the chamber. I will write all down:
Such, and such, pictures; there the window; and here,
Upon her arm—a bracelet! Come off, come off—
As slippery as the Gordian knot was hard!
Ah! 'Tis mine! I have enough:
To the trunk again, and shut the spring of it.
Swift, swift, you dragons of the night, that dawning
May bare the raven's eye! I lodge in fear;
Though this a heavenly angel, Hell is here.

[*A clock strikes.* IACHIMO *listens*]

ORLANDO: One, two, three: time, time!

[*He opens the lid of the trunk. Then, from out of the trunk, leaps the sinister figure of* LUKE. *He brandishes two large pistols—aiming them at the* KING *and* QUEEN. *Sensation!* ORLANDO *and all the ladies scream.* POTTS *pulls a sheet up over his head*]

LUKE: Nobody move! You, Nokes—out of my way! . . . Charles Stuart, I presume! [*He advances slowly towards the* KING. *The* KING *rises.* LUKE *cocks his pistols*]

LUKE: Your hour is come! Sic semper tyrannis!

[*But* ORLANDO, *furious, places himself between* LUKE *and the* KING]

ORLANDO: Now look here, Luke! I've had about enough of you . . . It's really too much.

LUKE: Out of my way!

ORLANDO: Never! Not only have you wasted a whole week of my time *and* ruined the greatest performance of my career. But you have lied to me.

LUKE: I warn you, Nokes.

ORLANDO: And I warn you that this time you've gone too far! You're supposed to be robbing the Mint, not holding up the plot and spoiling everyone's enjoyment.

LUKE: Then there's one bullet for *you*! And the second for the King!

[*But* ORLANDO *only smiles*]

ORLANDO: Very good. Bravo. . . but a little too late.

LUKE: What?

ORLANDO: Look behind you . . . No. Perhaps you'd better not.

LUKE: Who? What? Where?

ORLANDO: Behind you . . . All right, sir . . . Prince Rupert, isn't it? Didn't recognise you in this light . . . No, don't turn round, Ezekiel, old friend . . . The Prince has got a very nasty-looking sword pointing right at the back of your neck—I shouldn't look, if I were you! Whatever you do, don't turn round!

[*But* LUKE *is not convinced. He turns swiftly—to see nothing and nobody. As he turns,* ORLANDO *boots him in the back.* LUKE *falls on to his face and his pistols go off harmlessly and in the wrong direction.* LUKE *is seized by two burly* OFFICERS *and dragged away*]

ORLANDO: No Artist, and never will be!

KING CHARLES: Mr Nokes!

[ORLANDO *kneels*]

ORLANDO: Your Majesty. You must forgive me—

KING CHARLES: I think we should rather *thank* you.

ORLANDO: That villain said he was coming to rob your Mint—he never said anything about pistols and spoiling my exit. The trunk was supposed to be for the silver—not to hide in. I did try to tell the Dean, but he, poor fellow, is a trifle deaf.

KING: I know . . . But what of your fellow actors?

POTTS [*appearing from under the sheet*]: Please, your Majesty. Nothing to do with me, your Majesty.

ORLANDO: They *were* soldiers. But strictly between ourselves

—I can't think they were very good. . . . Given time, I might just make a passable troupe of Actors out of them. If they'd 'volunteer', that is.

POTTS: Oh, we'll volunteer all right, Mr Nokes. *All* of us will!

[*The Players appear round the bed and trunk—all rather sheepish*]

PLAYERS: Yes please, Mr Nokes . . . we'll all work very hard . . . we'd much rather Act than Fight . . .

ORLANDO [*dubious*]: Well . . .

POTTS: *Please,* Mr Nokes!

ORLANDO: Well . . . ? [*He looks at the* KING. KING CHARLES *nods*] All right . . . But any slacking and you'll go straight back to the Army—if they'll have you.

KING: That's settled then . . . Now, what about the rest of this play?

ORLANDO: The rest? You mean, you'd like us to go on?

KING: And why not?

ORLANDO: Why not indeed . . . Certainly, your Majesty! [*He bows. Then claps his hands*]. . . . Places, everybody!

[*The* KING *returns to his seat.* POTTS *settles back on the bed*]

ORLANDO: Now then . . . where was I?

QUEEN [*prompting*]: 'Swift, swift, you dragons of the night . . .'

ORLANDO [*overcome*]: Oh, thank you so much . . . Most kind . . . so very encouraging . . . thank you. . . . [*He returns to his position near the trunk. His audience settles down. Music . . .*]

ORLANDO [*as* IACHIMO]:

Swift, swift, you dragons of the night, that dawning
May bare the raven's eye! I lodge in fear;
Though this a heavenly angel, Hell is here.

[*The clock strikes*]

One, two, three: time! time!

[*He opens the lid of the trunk—and, this time, peers cautiously inside. It is empty.* ORLANDO *smiles at the audience, and then climbs in, closing the lid behind him. The* KING *and* QUEEN *lead an enthusiastic round of applause. The lid opens, and a delighted* ORLANDO *emerges to take a bow . . . At last, the lid closes and* ORLANDO *finally disappears . . . The play continues . . .*]

THE END

School Play

DONALD HOWARTH

CAST

TEACHER
STUDENTS

School Play

SCENE: *A group of* STUDENTS *is waiting for the teacher to arrive. Each student has a copy of this book. Some are already reading it, some have other interests and are reluctant to pay attention when the* TEACHER *enters. The* TEACHER *also has a copy of this book. He opens the book at this page. When the* TEACHER *thinks fit, he speaks.*

TEACHER: Now settle down, settle down . . .
[*They do*]
As I told you last time, we're going to read *School Play* today. [*He opens the book and finds the place*] It's by David—er—[*he checks to see*]—no, Donald Howarth and it's on page 133. So when you've all found it we'll begin.
[*The* STUDENTS *turn to this page in their books*]
As you see, there's a part for everyone so I don't have to cast it. We can all have a go at this one. There's even a part for me, unfortunately. This means it's going to be harder for me to direct when I'm in it as well. You'll have to watch what you're doing, more so than usual, as I'm likely to have problems of my own to sort out. The parts don't have names. They're numbered instead. But whenever there's a round bracket in a line of dialogue, it means you have to say the *real* name of whoever it is you're speaking to or about. If the round bracket refers to me, then you address me just as you normally would as 'Sir', not as TEACHER. So, we'll take the parts in turn as they come up on the page, starting at the back left with you (—) as ONE, (—) as TWO,

and so on until we get to you [*the last one in the group*] (—), then back to you, [*the first one in the group*] (—) and so on in rotation to the end. Anyway, the best thing is to work it out together as we go along. So let's see what happens.

[*Pause, during which* STUDENTS *and* TEACHER *read this sentence*]

Ready? [*The* TEACHER *looks up to see if they are*] Right, off you go then (—), with number ONE.

ONE [*doubtfully*]: Now—?

TEACHER: Yes.

[*Pause*]

ONE: It says ONE again, sir. Is it still me?

TEACHER: Er—yes, yes. That counts as a bit of dialogue between you and me: you not understanding, and me explaining.

TWO: You said we have to read it in turn one after the other off the page.

TEACHER: In most cases I think you'll find your cue will come from the same person—that is, the one on your right—*unless* a number is repeated when a bit of dialogue crops up, as it did just now between me and (ONE), or if I happen to say something or stop you, or . . . Surely that's plain enough? [*The* TEACHER *looks at* TWO *for agreement.* TWO *looks sceptically at* ONE *and then* THREE, *i.e., to the right and left of him*]
Oh, I'd better read the stage directions as well. 'The TEACHER looks at TWO for agreement. TWO looks sceptically at ONE and then THREE, that is, to the right and left of him.'

TWO: Is that in the play, though?

TEACHER: What?

TWO: You reading the directions like that?

TEACHER: If it's printed it's in.

TWO: Reading directions?

TEACHER: Yes.

TWO: But it spoils my part if you're going to read what I've just done.

TEACHER: Not necessarily.

TWO: You didn't read the stage directions at the beginning, did you?

TEACHER: No.

TWO: Why?

TEACHER: They weren't in the play.

TWO: They were printed.

TEACHER: Not for me to speak.

TWO: You said what was printed was in.

TEACHER [*vexed*]: All right, let's say I'll read them next time round, when we go through it again. (—), carry on with THREE, will you?

TWO [*aside to* ONE]: They shouldn't be read out loud.

THREE: I don't know what to say. [*Looks at* FOUR]

FOUR: Neither do I. [*Looks at* FIVE]

FIVE: Nor me. [*Looks at* SIX]

SIX [*looks up but says nothing*]

SEVEN [*to the* TEACHER]: How do I know when to say my line?

TEACHER: That's right. SIX has nothing to say, and you come in when you feel you should.

SEVEN: Can I go back and say it again then?

TEACHER: Yes, why not? Go back to THREE: 'I don't know what to say'.

THREE: Me?

TEACHER: Yes.

THREE: I don't know what to say. [*Looks at* FOUR]

FOUR: Neither do I. [*Looks at* FIVE]

FIVE: Nor me. [*Looks at* SIX]

SIX [*he doesn't speak*]

SEVEN: How do I know when to say my line?

[*General laughter.* EIGHT *doesn't laugh*]

EIGHT: Why can't I laugh?

NINE: You don't think it's funny.

TEN: You're humourless.

EIGHT: And you're stupid. What's so funny? There was nothing to laugh at anyway, so why did you?

TEACHER: That's enough now. Don't start quarrelling. Let's try and answer, shall we? Let's stick to the script. (EIGHT) asked two questions: 'Why did we laugh', and 'What was funny?'. [*Addressing* ELEVEN] (—), what did you think?'

ELEVEN: Well, it was SIX just sitting there not saying anything.

TWELVE: And SEVEN not knowing when to come in.

THIRTEEN: The way he said it.

FOURTEEN: The way he didn't say anything for so long.

TEACHER: But why was that funny?

FIFTEEN: Nobody knew what to do.

TEACHER: Is that funny? Not knowing what to do? [*The* TEACHER *scans the group*] How many of you think it was SIX's 'not saying anything' that was funny? Hands up.
[SIX *takes no part in the ballot. The* TEACHER *counts the hands and says how many*]
—[*the number counted*] How many of you think it was SEVEN's 'not knowing when to come in with the next line' that was funny? [*The* TEACHER *counts and says the number*] —. Hands up those who haven't put their hands up.
[*Hands go up*]
Those who didn't put their hands up: does that mean you didn't think there was anything to laugh at, or what?
[*Here follow the explanations of those who raised their hands in response to the* TEACHER's *last question. What is said is written down and put into the play. The* TEACHER *might use blackboard and chalk*]

TEACHER: Fine. Now, just to recap, we have — [*the first figure*] who thought SIX's not saying anything was funny;— [*the second figure*] who laughed at SEVEN's not knowing when to say the next line; and — [*the third figure*] who didn't . . .

SIXTEEN [*cutting in*] So what?

SEVENTEEN: So nothing.

EIGHTEEN: Just more teaching.

NINETEEN: Yeah . . . Why don't you ask SIX why he didn't say anything, instead of having votes on it? I mean, if he'd said something we wouldn't have had to laugh, and you wouldn't have asked us why, and all that.

TWENTY: Yes . . . It's not our fault SIX didn't say anything.

TWENTY-ONE: Who wants to know why we laughed, or didn't, anyway?

TWENTY-TWO: Not me.

TWENTY-THREE: Nor me.

TWENTY-FOUR: Me neither.

TWENTY-FIVE: Neither do I.

TEACHER: Wait a minute; not so fast; think what you're saying. First, NINETEEN, you don't know whether you'd have laughed or not if SIX had spoken. He might have said something amusing. And second, you really mustn't make it sound as though it were all my fault. I didn't start this thing so I can't be expected to go on as I would have meant to if I had. As your teacher, I'm not responsible for anything any of you are made to do or say any more than *you* are. I don't make things up as I go along any more than any of you. I'm not to blame. Even if I am, I'm not. Moroever, I'm not responsible for anything I'm made to say or do, either. I'm doing my bit, playing my part as best I can like everybody else. [*After a short pause, recovering*] To be quite frank with you, I'm on your side. I don't want to know why some of you were supposed to have giggled—or didn't —either, any more than any of you did. I was just playing my part in the scheme of things . . . in the play, I mean . . .

TWENTY-SIX: You like to find things out, though, don't you?

TWENTY-SEVEN: Yeah, and you chose to be the teacher, you took it for granted.

TWENTY-EIGHT: We're just numbers.

TWENTY-NINE: Why can't one of *us* play the teacher's part?

THIRTY: It's bigger than any of ours.

TEACHER: Would you like to, (TWENTY-NINE)?

TWENTY-NINE: I'm not old enough.

[*General laughter*]

TEACHER: I won't ask why you thought that was funny . . . but as we've got this far we may as well go on. Let's go back to NINETEEN'S suggestion: that we should ask you, SIX, why you didn't say anything. Can you tell us?
[*Pause*]
Why do you think SIX wasn't given anything to say?
[*Pause. The* TEACHER *turns back the pages of the book to check* FIVE'S *earlier line*].
Why do you think SIX didn't have a line after FIVE said 'Nor me'?
[*By now the group is focussing on* SIX]
You can speak now. I'm asking you as your teacher on behalf of us all. Why do you think you won't co-operate? Come along! Who has the next line?

THIRTY-ONE: Me.

TEACHER: You ask.

THIRTY-ONE [*to* SIX]: Why didn't you say something?

TEACHER: Well, SIX? You've heard of the gentle art of improvisation—spontaneity—? Let's have a bit of it now. It's up to each of us to bring something of our own to bear on what's going on.

THIRTY-THREE: But he can't, sir. There's nothing written in for SIX to speak.

TEACHER: That's not a good enough reason for his obstinate silence. He can speak without having a written answer. He's sabotaging the whole play.

THIRTY-FOUR: But this play isn't like a play. We don't have parts like we usually do.

TWENTY-EIGHT: I said we're just numbers.

THIRTY-FIVE: We don't have any characters to be.

THIRTY-SIX: We're only ourselves.

TEACHER: Very well then. Be anyone you want to be. Ignore what's printed on the page and make your own lines up. We'll start at the top with you, (ONE). Say anything you like.

ONE: Anything you like.

TEACHER [*ironically*]: Brilliant. (TWO), you can beat that, can't you?

TWO: If I make up a line, how will the audience know I have?

TEACHER: Because we've already told them that's what we're doing.

THREE: But do you think they'll believe us?

TEACHER: If you're sincere, yes. Come along, (FOUR), say a line.

FOUR [*He actually makes up a line*]

TEACHER: Very good. Write it down. Next.

FIVE [*He also makes up a line*]

TEACHER: Good. Write it down. Next.

SIX [*He doesn't say anything*]

TEACHER: Well, SIX? It's your turn to contribute. You're keeping us waiting. What's the matter? Very well, you leave us no alternative. If you want to be on your own, sticking out like a sore thumb in a minority—you must expect to be treated like one. It might be different if you were a hero in some way, or loyal to a cause we agreed with, or if you'd managed to do something that had merit in our eyes which set you apart from the rest of us. But you've done nothing. You've said nothing. We won't have that. Plain silence compels us to express ourselves vociferously, with contempt and derision as far as the regulations allow. Everybody stand up. [*They do*] Everybody sit except SIX. [*Everyone obeys*] Those who have nothing written down in the book to speak and who refuse to say anything of their own, and those who make everybody stand up and sit down again to draw attention to themselves, are excluded. Those who kindly remain seated will now come here to me. Gather round.
[*The* GROUP *obeys.* SIX *is isolated*]
Come along quickly. That's right, good. Speaking from left to right, what should be done with SIX in the circumstances? Name and choose the alternatives.

[*The* GROUP *speaks from left to right, facing* SIX]

FIRST: Leave him alone.

SECOND: Bash him.

THIRD: Kick him.

FOURTH: Lock him up.

FIFTH: Let him off.

SIXTH: Not without a fair trial.

SEVENTH: Yeah. Who are you, SIX?

EIGHTH: Where d'you come from, SIX?

NINTH: When's your birthday, SIX?

TENTH: What's your number, SIX?

ELEVENTH: SIX is it, SIX?

TWELFTH: Want to get done in outside, SIX?

THIRTEENTH: Behind a wall in the yard?

FOURTEENTH: Or up on the hill.

FIFTEENTH: For your very own good, SIX, in the long run.

SIXTEENTH: Would you like to be done?

SEVENTEENTH: Say 'yes', or else . . .

[*Pause*]

EIGHTEENTH: We'll have to force the words out.

NINETEENTH: Yeah. Not saying anything gives him the best part.

TWENTIETH: Yeah. We're the ones who do all the work.

TWENTY-FIRST: All the learning.

TWENTY-SECOND: The acting.

TWENTY-THIRD: The feeling the lines.

TWENTY-FOURTH: All for SIX, who says nothing.

TWENTY-FIFTH: And gets his own way.

TWENTY-SIXTH: And all the sympathy, too.

TWENTY-SEVENTH: All except ours.

TWENTY-EIGHTH: Let's cut his part out for his own good.

TWENTY-NINTH: For good.

THIRTIETH: Make up another.

THIRTY-FIRST: Those who won't join in, keep out.

THIRTY-SECOND: We're in charge of the way things are.

THIRTY-THIRD: Take hold of his book.

THIRTY-FOURTH: Don't let him read on.

THIRTY-FIFTH [*taking the book from* SIX]: Now you're not one of us.

THIRTY-SIXTH: It's for your own good.

THIRTY-SEVENTH: In the long run.

THIRTY-EIGHTH: Lost the power of speech, SIX?

THIRTY-NINTH: Lost your tongue, SIX?

FORTIETH: You're too late, SIX.

FORTY-FIRST: You're out of bounds, SIX.

FORTY-SECOND: Trespassing, SIX.

FORTY-THIRD: Better for your own good, for good, SIX.

FORTY-FOURTH: You're a number in name only now.

FORTY-FIFTH: Nobody.

FORTY-SIXTH: Nowhere.

FORTY-SEVENTH: Nothing else.

FORTY-EIGHTH: SIX is nothing, SIX.

FORTY-NINTH: Say that in your witness box.

FIFTIETH: Nothing changes our verdict.

FIFTY-FIRST: No-one listens to anonymous.

FIFTY-SECOND: Are you married?

FIFTY-THIRD: Who's your father?

FIFTY-FOURTH: What's the matter?

FIFTY-FIFTH: Hurry up.

FIFTY-SIXTH: Find out.

FIFTY-SEVENTH: Like it.

FIFTY-EIGHTH: Lump it.

FIFTY-NINTH
SIXTIETH
SIXTY-FIRST } [*together*]: Stop your ears.
Shut your eyes.
Sink or swim.

[*Pause*]

SIXTY-SECOND: We've done you now.

TEACHER: Oh well done, everyone, well done. Thank you. Next time through we'll try it with a scream right at the end and make everyone feel we've really told SIX where to get off for his own sake. I think we might have him standing up on something and you all crowd in like a rugby scrum until SIX topples backwards, arms akimbo, vanquished. Splendid.

[SIX *puts his hand up*]

Yes, (SIX)?

SIX [*learnt*]: Please may I leave the room?

TEACHER: Very well, but don't be long.

[*Another student puts his hand up*]

STUDENT [*learnt*]: Can I go too?

TEACHER: Yes, but hurry up. You're the last one. Anyone else must wait until the bell goes. I want to go over what we've done before going on to the end.
[SIX *and the other student leave the room*]
Now, back to your places everyone. Take up your positions as you were to begin with.
[*The* GROUP *does so*]
I'll read the opening stage directions before I leave you, as I said I would, for your benefit, (TWO). A group of students is waiting for the teacher to arrive. Each student has a copy of this book. Some are already reading it, some have other interests and are reluctant to pay attention when the teacher enters. The teacher also has a copy of this book. He opens the book at this page. When the teacher thinks fit, he speaks. So, when (SIX) and (the STUDENT) come back, I'll go out and come in again, and we'll see how much we've remembered.
[*Pause. The* TEACHER *checks the time. The* STUDENT

returns. He carries a piece of toilet-paper with something written on it]
You've kept us waiting, (STUDENT).

STUDENT: Sorry.

TEACHER: Where's (SIX)?

STUDENT: He's dead, sir. Outside, sir.

TEACHER: Are you sure?

STUDENT: Yes, sir. He asked me to give you this.

TEACHER: Did you wash your hands?

STUDENT: Yes.

[*The* TEACHER *takes the paper and glances at it*]

TEACHER: Go back to your place and let's get started again.
[*The* STUDENT *goes back to his seat. The* TEACHER *goes to the door and speaks from there*]
I'm going to make my entrance. I'll count ten from the opening.
[*The* TEACHER *exits. The* GROUP *carries out the opening stage directions as before. The* TEACHER *re-enters*]

TEACHER: Now settle down, settle down.
[*They do*]
As I told you last time, we're going to read *School Play* today. It's on page 133. When you've all found it, we'll begin.
[*The* STUDENTS *turn to this page in their books*]
As you'll see, there's a part for everyone, so I don't have to cast it. We can all have a go. The parts don't have names, they're numbered, so we'll take them in turn as they come up on the page, starting at the back left with you, (—), as

ONE, (—) as TWO, etc. For the rest, we'll work it out as we go along and see what happens. Ready?
[*The* TEACHER *looks up to see if they are*]
Right, off you go then, (—), with number ONE.

ONE [*doubtfully*]: Now—?

TEACHER: Yes.

ONE [*after a short pause*]: It says ONE again, sir. Is it still me?

TEACHER: Er—yes, yes. That counts as a bit of dialogue between you and me, you not understanding and me explaining.

TWO: You said we had to read in turn one after the other off the page.

TEACHER: In most cases I think you'll find your cue will come from the same person—that is, the one on your right—unless a number is repeated when a bit of dialogue crops up as it did just now between me and (ONE), or if I happen to say something or stop you, or . . . Surely that's plain enough?
[TWO *looks sceptically at* ONE]
(—), carry on with THREE will you?

THREE: I don't know what to say. [*Looks at* FOUR]

FOUR: Neither do I. [*Looks at* FIVE]

FIVE: Nor me. [*Looks at the empty place beside him*]

ORIGINAL SEVEN: There's no SIX, sir. How do I know when to say my line?

TEACHER: SIX has nothing to say. Just speak when you feel you should, as you did last time.

SEVEN: I can't.

TEACHER: SIX is no longer with us.

SEVEN: I can't be SEVEN if there isn't any SIX.

TEACHER: Would you like to be SIX?

SEVEN: No sir.

TEACHER: Carry on then.

SEVEN: Where from?

TEACHER: Where you left off.

SEVEN [*flatly*]: How do I know when to say my line?

[*Nobody laughs*]

EIGHT: Sir, if nobody laughs there it won't make sense if I say 'Why can't I laugh?'.

NINE: Now I can't say my line, can I?

TEN: What about mine?

TEACHER: If only you'd stick to the script and say what you said before, I might be able to say my lines without having to keep changing them and making amendments to adjust to the ever-increasing need . . . demands you make . . . If you're not going to laugh, how can I ask you what you thought was funny?

ELEVEN: I should say SIX sitting there not saying anything was funny . . .

TEACHER [*showing signs of desperation*]: Who took (SIX'S) book from him?
[*The* STUDENT *who did puts his hand up*]
Go and sit between (FIVE) and (SEVEN).

THE STUDENT: But what about my lines I said before?

TEACHER: Someone else will say them when the time comes. No-one's indispensable.

THE STUDENT: SIX is.

TEACHER: You're SIX.

THE STUDENT: What happens next time round? You'll have to replace me when I die like (ORIGINAL SIX) did, and soon there won't be enough . . .

TEACHER: I don't know . . . I'm confused . . . Let's stop it. I can't go on any more . . . not if you won't say what was written down before . . . Either we continue as we were with someone else being as stubborn as SIX, or we give up . . . I can't think and act . . . It's too much on top of all things considered . . . I have problems enough at home . . . my private life and the political situation . . . I can't be exploited . . . The Committee wants to know . . . books to mark . . . I must read the papers and there are games to attend to with loved ones . . . Not enough time to go on holiday for a while . . . Break down the barriers into component parts and the system . . . Energy is involved, chasing rewards . . . wasted effort . . . endeavouring . . . contrary to common belief . . . contrary to our expectations . . . Future prospects difficult to forecast in the long term . . . Notwithstanding . . . when all's said and done . . . Apologise . . . Pay attention . . . Carry on without . . . Give over . . . Never mind . . . Never, never, mind . . .

[*The* TEACHER *mumbles into silence and sits huddled up with head in hands, rocking gently backwards and forwards. The* GROUP *is silent for a while and shows a tendency to titter. Soon the* STUDENT *next to the* STUDENT-WHO-FOLLOWED-SIX-TO-THE-LAVATORY *speaks*]

STUDENT: What did it say on that piece of paper?

[*The* STUDENT *addressed leans over and whispers into his neighbour's ear. Soon the whole* GROUP *is receiving the message as it is passed round. They become more rowdy and disorganised, each reacting differently to the passed-on information. A school bell is rung to denote the end of the period. The* GROUP *scrambles to its feet, gathering books and schoolbags as if preparing to go to another class. The* TEACHER *is still in a state of nervous collapse. Pause. The* ORIGINAL SIX *returns and goes to his desk. The* GROUP *freezes. He takes his book out and picks up a school satchel. He looks at the* TEACHER *curiously, and slowly goes up to him*]

SIX: Sir. The bell rang sir. [*Pause*] The lesson's over, sir. [*Pause*] What's the matter? Why don't you say something? [*Pause*] The play's finished so you don't have to read it, sir. Say something, sir, won't you? Please? Please say something. Speak to me. [*Shaking the* TEACHER *gently by the arm*] Say something . . . please . . . say something . . .

[*But the* TEACHER *is silent*]

THE END